co/aa

4 Y

95 96
    97

D1357016

WITHD

008537

Past-into-Present Series

Radicals and Reformers

Peter Lane

Principal Lecturer in History,
Coloma College of Education

B. T. BATSFORD LTD   London

Acknowledgments

The author and publishers would like to thank the following for the illustrations in this book: The Anti-Apartheid Movement for fig. 63; the BBC for fig. 2; the British Museum for figs. 6 and 9; Camera Press for figs. 59 and 64; Central Press Photos for fig. 4; Fox Photos for fig. 55; Glasgow Herald for fig. 60; the Imperial War Museum for fig. 3; Keystone Press for figs. 57, 58, 61 and 62; the Mansell Collection for figs. 29, 33, 34 and 42–44; the Middleton Library for fig. 18; the National Portrait Gallery for figs. 15, 16, 22, 27 and 38; Radio Times Hulton Picture Library for figs. 1, 19, 21, 23, 25, 28, 32, 35, 37, 38, 45, 47, 49–53 and 56; Topix for fig. 54.

First published 1973
© Peter Lane 1973

Filmset by Keyspools Ltd, Golborne, Lancashire

Printed in Great Britain by
The Anchor Press Ltd, Tiptree, Essex
for the Publishers
B. T. BATSFORD Ltd, 4 Fitzhardinge Street, London W1V 0AH

ISBN 0 7134 1782 X

Contents

The Illustrations

1 Radicals and their Methods

This picture was taken just over one hundred years ago, when many thousands of children worked from an early age in brickyards, engineering works or shops, or tried to earn a living selling matches, laces or flowers from street-stalls. This was long after the early Factory Acts had forbidden employers to use child labour in mines and cotton mills. Some history books suggest that after about 1850 no children went to work in industrialised Britain. This picture shows that for some children this was not so.

1 Children at work in a brickfield in the 1870s. This was one of the dirty and dangerous jobs which many Victorian children had to do long after the Factory Acts forbade their employment in textile mills and coal mines.

Today we know that it does not happen; everyone has to stay at school until they are sixteen years old, and about half the nation's children stay on at school after that age to get one or other of the many qualifications which will help them to get a better job when they leave school. We would be horrified if anyone suggested that ten-year-old boys and girls should leave school to work in a brick-yard where they would carry heavy lumps of wet clay.

There has been a great change in people's ideas of how children should be treated. There have been other similarly great changes in people's ideas of how we should treat old people, the sick, and the unemployed; in the past these less well-off members of society were treated as though their misfortunes were their fault and nothing to do with the rest of us. Today we expect the government, acting on our behalf, to collect taxes and give help to the less well-off.

Radical change

There are different ways in which our lives may change; some of us may be affected by an alteration to the bus timetable; others may be annoyed by a ban on

2 A music and movement lesson in a modern primary school. These children will not be asked to go to work until they are at least sixteen – unlike their early Victorian counterparts.

3 Russian soldiers and sailors fighting the Tsar's loyal forces during the 1917 Revolution. Radicals are not revolutionaries; they do not call for violent action such as this nor do they call for the overthrow of the political system of the country in which they live.

car-parking in some favourite spot. These and similar changes in our day-to-day lives are only small, and our lives go on much as before. But the way in which we treat children today, compared with the way in which they were treated in the past, is a very great change and different altogether from the small changes mentioned above. Such great changes deserve the name *radical* changes because they completely alter the pattern of people's lives; they get to the root (or *radex* in Latin) and basically (or *at the roots*) alter people's lives.

One is entitled to ask, 'Why, after hundreds of years during which children worked, did the government decide to change the law and compel children to attend school?' Or again, 'Why, after centuries during which women had been regarded as inferior to men, did opinion change, so that to-day women are regarded as men's equals?' Why, in fact, do great changes take place? One answer is that a number of people begin to ask for the change. People, who are unwilling to accept life as it is, and ask that changes should be made, are called *radicals*. They are not revolutionaries – who use violence and force to overthrow one type of government in order to put another in its place. The radical does not want, for example, to kill the monarch, as did the French Revolutionaries; he does not propose the overthrow of a government and its replacement by a Party dictatorship, as did the Russian Bolshevik Revolutionaries. The radical believes that the country in which he is living, its government, its way of life is very good – apart from the evil which he proposes to change. After he has succeeded, for

7

4 Lloyd George, electioneering in 1924. In 1909 he had proposed increasing taxes paid by the well-to-do in order to pay for the infant Welfare State. The rich man was not ruined because of Lloyd George's proposals; indeed there are more rich people today than there were in 1909.

example, in getting the vote for women, or pensions for old people, the life of the country goes on much as before, except that the country and people have accepted the change.

Radical methods

How do radicals go about persuading their fellow countrymen and, in particular, the government that their ideas are good? We will see that, in general, all radicals have used the same sorts of weapons in their fight; they have been all great orators and could get a crowd of people worked up. Hunt (Chapter 3) attracted crowds of over 40,000 to meetings called in London and Manchester. Lord Shaftesbury (Chapter 5) spoke so movingly about the plight of children working in mines that he had even hardened MPs weeping. Lloyd George and Joseph Chamberlain (Chapter 7), Richard Cobden and Mrs Pankhurst (Chapters 4 and 8), were all great orators.

But the radicals realised that they could only convince a small number of people by their speeches; they could never hope to speak to all the people in the country. They also realised that while the mob may roar its approval of a speaker, the mob may also forget very quickly what he has said. So all radical movements have also concentrated on printed propaganda; Cobbett's *Political Register*, Wilkes's *North Briton*, Fergus O'Connor's *Northern Star* are the predecessors of the radical papers of our own time, with their off-beat titles such as *Black Dwarf*, *Oz* and so on.

In their papers and speeches the radicals have always tried to do two things. First, they have ridiculed the opposition to change. In poems, songs, cartoons and reports of speeches, the radical has always tried to get the mass of people to laugh at the opposition. 'Nothing succeeds like ridicule' seems to be a radical slogan. On the other hand, the radical has also tried to show how evil the opposition is. Shelley's poetry (Chapter 3) and Bertrand Russell's attacks on Macmillan and the H-Bomb (Chapter 10) are only two examples.

5 Among the ruins of a village a Vietnamese searches for her family belongings. Revolution, riots and war bring disasters such as this; the radical asks for peaceful change.

Ridicule and attack are the two weapons used by radicals in their campaigns. How do governments, employers and other people react to these attacks? Here again there seems to be a pattern. At first the government tends to ignore the speeches, articles, cartoons and so on – rather as if they were saying 'Don't pay any attention and the thing will go away'. When the attacks continue, the tendency is for authority to over-react: they ordered a military attack on a mob at Peterloo (Chapter 3); they ordered the forcible feeding of women prisoners (Chapter 8); they tried to supress the speakers such as Wilkes (Chapter 2) and the newspapers such as the *Political Register*; they imprisoned Chartist leaders (Chapter 6).

At first sight one might think that this is the way to treat a nuisance such as a radical demanding great changes. In fact, such treatment only calls attention to the radical and to his campaign; the cruel treatment of suffragette prisoners (Chapter 8) roused the conscience of people who might otherwise never have become interested in the question of women's emancipation. Indeed, there is some evidence that radicals have gone out of their way to attract a violent reaction from government in order that their message might be got across to a wider public, which is drawn to sympathy with their cause as a result of government reaction.

The work of a number of radicals is examined in the following pages. There were, of course, many other radicals whose work was as important as that of the ones dealt with here. Unfortunately there is insufficient room, so that many outstanding people have had to be excluded. However, those who have been included cover a variety of causes and careers, and all serve to illustrate the way in which radical movements arise, develop and end.

2 Wilkes and Liberty

Dickens called the eighteenth century 'the best of times and the worst of times'. One of those whose career brings out both the best and worst of that century is John Wilkes. Born in 1727 he first became famous as a wild-living and immoral member of the Hell-Fire Club, a club founded by Sir Francis Dashwood, the owner of a huge estate at West Wycombe. In 1752 Dashwood had bought Medmenham Abbey, 6 miles (10 km) away from his estate, where he and his friends, the Marquess of Bute, the Earl of Sandwich, John Wilkes, and other rakes of the period held nightly sessions of Black Magic and orgies which a Club member, William Hogarth, has commemorated in *The Rake's Progress* and *The Harlot's Progress*.

6 *The Rake's Progress* by Hogarth. Many rich young men of the eighteenth century supported liberty (see the banners) as part of their desire for freedom to live as they pleased. The artist did not think very much of these debauchers, drunkards, and libertines.

In between designing the rebuilt abbey and organising the Club's immoral activities, Dashwood, Bute and Sandwich were also MPs. Wilkes was elected MP for Aylesbury in 1757. Like most other MPs he had used corrupt methods to be elected; getting his borough cost him £7,000 – almost the whole of his wife's fortune.

George III

In 1760 George II died and his grandson succeeded to the throne. Unlike the first two Hanoverian Kings, he had been born in England and boasted that he was English. His mother had appointed the Marquess of Bute as tutor to the young Prince, and there is a good deal of evidence that she also appointed herself mistress of this noble member of the Hell-Fire Club.

One of George III's ambitions was 'to be a King' – unlike the first two Georges who had allowed the Whig aristocracy to grow more powerful, appoint the Ministers and to take away their power. George III dismissed the popular Pitt from office and appointed his former tutor, Bute, as Prime Minister. He, in turn, promoted Dashwood to be Chancellor of the Exchequer, but did not make his friend Wilkes Governor of Canada, as Wilkes had expected. He never forgave Bute.

7 The punning symbol for Bute was the jackboot, here seen to contain George III's mother and her supposed lover, the Marquess of Bute. The white horse and zebra represented King George III and his Queen and the Scottish driver is urging them to make a peace with France. The Scottish appearance of the driver and other figures was meant to be a sneer at the Scottish Marquess.

Dashwood was not a successful Chancellor; his most famous mistake was to impose a new tax on cyder. Neither was Bute a very successful Prime Minister, as is shown by one of the popular songs of the time:

> The King was going to Parliament,
> A numerous crowd was round him,
> Some huzza'd him as he went,
> And others cry'd – confound him!
> At length a shout – came thundering out!
> Which made the air to ring, Sir,
> All in one voice – cry'd no excise,
> NO BUTE, no Cyder King, Sir.

Wilkes and his friend Charles Churchill had founded a newspaper called *The North Briton* – a slur on the Scottish Marquess of Bute, whom they attacked continually in the early numbers of their paper. In Number 5, for example, they told the story of Bute's affairs with the King's mother. But it was because of Number 45 that Wilkes earned for himself a place in history. This appeared in 1763 after the government, under Bute, had made peace with France and so abandoned the King of Prussia, our ally, who had no warning that Britain was to make peace with France, and was therefore forced to fight on his own.

8 Bute was unpopular because of the Peace with France but his unpopularity increased when he introduced a tax on cider in March 1763. The head of the knave is meant to be a reflection of the people's opinion of Bute; the setting sun represents the window tax and the ground at the exciseman's feet represents the Land Tax. Bute resigned in April 1763 in the face of such opposition.

Wilkes and Parliament

Wilkes wrote about the King's speech on the opening of Parliament

... I am sure all foreigners, especially the King of Prussia, will hold the minister in contempt and abhorrence. He has made our Sovereign declare: 'My expectations have been fully answered by the happy effects which the several allies of my Crown have derived from this salutary measure of the definitive treaty. The powers at war with my good brother the King of Prussia have been induced to agree to such terms as that great Prince has approved'. The infamous fallacy of this whole sentence is apparent to all mankind. . . . No advantage has accrued to that magnanimous Prince from our negotiation, but he was basely deserted by the Scottish Prime Minister of England.

Later on in the article he appealed to the public not to let the country rest in the hands of these friends of the King who would destroy all liberal institutions. Public reaction was violent; the mob burned jackboots in the streets (Bute's name was pronounced 'boot'), together with petticoats – a reflection on the memory of the King's mother. The King decided to get rid of the man who called him a liar. Because the offending article was not signed, there was no proof that Wilkes had written it; the King forced the government to issue a 'general warrant' for the arrest of everyone connected with the *North Briton* – publishers, printers, editors and workpeople. The 'general warrant' was, in fact, quite a dangerous weapon,

9 John Wilkes, drawn by Hogarth in May 1763. Hogarth hated Wilkes who, he said, only pretended to be 'a Brutus a saviour of his country'. 4,000 copies of this print were sold in a few weeks. Wilkes appears to be a devilishly cunning schemer with his *North Briton* papers beside him and his dunce's cap of liberty almost covering his horned wig.

since it allowed the King to arrest almost anyone thought to be associated with a criminal act without having to have evidence against him.

When Wilkes was arrested and thrown into the Tower of London the London mob rioted in defence of 'Wilkes and Liberty'; noblemen were dragged from their sedan chairs and rolled in the gutter and '45' was chalked on the soles of their shoes. The King was pelted with rotten fruit when he appeared. The Lord Chief Justice heard the case against Wilkes and agreed with him that as an MP and a reporter he had the right to comment on the government's activities. Wilkes was released, even more a radical hero because he had proved the King to be a liar (in Number 45) and a tyrant who had acted illegally in arresting him. Even when the King released Wilkes, the clamour continued. The Marquess of Bute was nearly killed when he was mobbed as he entered Parliament; when the King went riding in his royal coach the mob smashed the windows. The King decided that if he could not punish Wilkes for the publication of the *North Briton* he would find another excuse for arresting the leader of the people.

On 15 November 1763 Wilkes's former friend, the Earl of Sandwich – a member of the government and a friend of the King – read out in Parliament the *Essay on Woman* – a filthy parody of Pope's *Essay on Man*, which Wilkes had composed for the pleasure of the members of the Hell-Fire Club, including the Earl of Sandwich. The poem was produced as evidence that Wilkes was guilty of blasphemy and of circulating indecent literature. The Commons voted by a majority of 44 that Wilkes was guilty, and he was declared an outlaw. But he had guessed what the verdict would be and had fled to France.

In 1768 Wilkes, still an outlaw, returned from France and announced that he would be a candidate at the General Election. He was invited to stand for Middlesex, then a constituency where many hundreds of people voted. This made it difficult for anyone to use the usual methods of bribing the voters; it also meant that Wilkes could use his popularity with the mob to good effect. To guarantee he had their support, Wilkes forced the warden of the King's Bench prison to take him into the gaol as the publisher of an obscure poem. The mob, believing that he had been arrested by the unpopular government of George III, rioted. During the riots outside the prison (10 May 1768) the troops were beaten and stoned. A young man, William Allen, was chased by three soldiers and shot. The soldiers happened to be Scottish and the affair was portrayed in cartoons and poems as an attempt by Bute to attack the liberties of Englishmen. The magistrate who gave the order to fire was tried for murder – so that magistrates in 1780 (at the time of the Gordon Riots) were unwilling to give such orders.

Wilkes was duly elected MP for Middlesex, but the King persuaded Parliament to vote that he should not be allowed to take his seat since he was a traitor, a blasphemer and a writer of immoral poems. The election had to be held again; and on this and on a third occasion, Wilkes won. However, Parliament decided to seat his opponent, Lutrell, even though Wilkes had gained 1,143 votes to his 296. This led to agitation concerning the rights of electors to decide who their MP

THE SCOTCH VICTORY

To the Earl of ___ Protector of our Liberties this Plate is Humbly Inscribed by L. Junius Brutus &c

10 During riots outside the King's Bench prison where Wilkes was under arrest the troops were stoned and mobbed. A young man, William Allen, was chased by three soldiers and shot on 10 May 1768. The soldiers were Scottish and the affair was treated as an attack on English liberties planned and directed by Bute, the King and the Scottish soldiers.

was to be, and when Wilkes was finally allowed to take his seat this issue had been decided in favour of the people and against the King.

Meanwhile he continued to attack the King. In his *Letters to Junius* (1769) he wrote to the King:

'Sir – It is the misfortune of your life, and originally the cause of every reproach and distress which has attended your government, that you should never have been acquainted with truth until you heard it in the complaints of your people. It is not, however, too late to correct the error of your education. We are still inclined to make allowance for the lessons you received in your youth. . . . We separate the amiable prince from the treachery of his servants . . .'.

His campaign attracted others to write. A *New Song* for Wilkes's birthday in 1769 begins:

> Here's a Health to our King,
> Let's rejoice and Sing,
> And may he grow wiser and wiser;
> And may he grow wiser and wiser;
> And wise he'd now be,
> Were it not for a she,
> And a damnable Scottish adviser.

Wilkes and America

The conflict between Wilkes and George III's government began in 1763 with the publication of Number 45 of the *North Briton*. But George III's government was the government that was responsible for the American colonies. Bute's successor, Grenville, was the Minister responsible for the passing of the Stamp Act by which the British government tried to impose taxes on the unwilling colonists. Pitt, for the moment an opponent of George III, became a friend of Wilkes – also an opponent to the King. The politicians and the mob who cried 'Wilkes and Liberty' were quite easily persuaded to add 'and no taxation without representation' to their list of anti-government slogans.

Benjamin Franklin, the colonists' representative in England, became a member of the Hell-Fire Club and persuaded Dashwood – no longer a Minister – and Wilkes to take up the cause of the colonists. Wilkes became the London representative of the Sons of Liberty and was in constant touch with leading figures in the colonies. In 1769 this importance was indicated when a new town in Pennsylvania was named Wilkes-Barre.

Few people in the colonies wanted to break with England; right up to the Declaration of Independence (July 1776) most leaders hoped that the King would be made to see the stupidity of his American policy. Wilkes led deputations of English merchants and MPs to see the King, to ask that he reverse his policy. In

11 *The Parricide* was drawn in 1776 and shows America as an Indian woman attacking Britannia. Wilkes, pointing towards Britannia, is directing the 'Indian' attack while Chatham and Fox (represented by the fox in the background) look on at the murder of their country.

1775 Parliament voted to send an army to put down the first stirrings of military revolt; Wilkes, since 1774 an Alderman of London, protested: 'This is a revolution, not a rebellion. Who knows whether in consequence of this day's mad address, in a few years the independent Americans may not celebrate 1775 as we do the revolution of 1688.' The Commons laughed him down; not for the last time the radical was to have the last laugh.

Wilkes had been a friend of the Elder Pitt, whose son was appointed Prime Minister by George III in 1783. The appointment was unpopular with the leading politicians of all parties; Wilkes, as if to be contrary, favoured this promotion of his former friend's son. George III welcomed this unlooked-for support for his nominee; in 1784 he allowed Wilkes to take his seat in the Commons. Now Wilkes himself became the object of attack from the radical cartoonists and poets; they

12 *The Hanoverian Horse and the British Lion* drawn in March 1784. The Younger Pitt is riding the horse, which represents the King, and is about to attack Fox, riding the British Lion. The horse is also kicking at the House of Commons, its feet planted on Magna Carta, the Bill of Rights and 'Constitution'; Fox wants Pitt to dismount and allow him, as Prime Minister, to ride the horse. Pitt and the King dissolved Parliament and held a General Election in which Pitt defeated the Foxites and strengthened his position.

were anxious for Parliamentary reform and saw in Young Pitt an obstacle to their demands. One attack on Wilkes read:

When Piety and Blasphemy agree,
Can there a stranger Coalition be!
'O best of Kings!' cried Wilkes, 'for ever live',
'Subjects like Wilkes', says George, 'kind of fortune give!'

Significance of Wilkes

As a result of his earlier struggles against the King, Wilkes proved the illegality of the use of general warrants and also established the freedom of the Press. Also as a result of his earlier campaigns Wilkes became an ally of Wyvill and other radicals who demanded reform of Parliament (Chapter 3), and his struggle with the King strengthened the case for such reform.

His newspaper and poems, the cartoons of his friends and supporters, his rallying of the mob and his adoption of the American cause, enlivened the political scene in England at the end of the eighteenth century and served as a model for subsequent radical campaigns against oppression. However, as the ageing, debauched friend of the King whom he had once despised, he serves also as a reminder of how men change their opinions as they get older; the radical of one generation may well become the conservative of the next, out of touch with the new radicals and their demands for reform.

3 Orator Hunt

Changing England

Henry Hunt was born in 1773, the son of a Wiltshire farmer. While he was growing up the face of England was changing as both agriculture and industry went through the beginnings of their revolutions. Farmers were beginning to use new and more efficient machines; Bakewell and the Colling brothers showed the farmers the advantages of stock breeding; Townshend and other Norfolk farmers had shown how land and stock could be improved by the use of root crops and Arthur Young was spending his time travelling around the country writing reports of the changes he had seen, and advising the farmers he visited to change their methods of farming.

Hunt saw something of these changes in Wiltshire. He did not see the beginnings of the Industrial Revolution which was centred on the cotton industry of Lancashire, the coal industry of South Wales and the North East, and the iron industry of Shropshire. Villages became towns and towns became cities as factories were built, mines opened and ironworks established. Although the majority of the English people continued to live in the countryside, even by 1800 – when Hunt was beginning to take an interest in political affairs – there was an increasing number of English people living in the new towns. Here the owners of industries and banks, of shipyards and canals, of mines and ironworks, grew rich; rich on a scale that no townspeople had ever dreamt of before. They made their money at the expense

13 Orator Hunt, one of the leading radicals in the years of unrest 1815–22. A member of the middle class, he demanded Parliamentary reform as a path to economic and social reforms.

14 The Wedgwood family. Josiah Wedgwood was the founder of the famous pottery firm. The painting illustrates the way in which some industrialists had copied the aristocracy in their style of life; they also wanted a share in the aristocracy's political power.

of their workers who worked long hours, earned low wages and lived in appalling conditions – so that over half their children died before they reached the age of five, while the average age of death for the working class was only fifteen. William Cobbett, writing in his radical paper, *The Political Register*, noted: 'When master and man were the terms, every one was in his place and all were free. Now, in fact, it is an affair of masters and slaves.' Cobbett was a romantic radical; he believed that there had once been a golden age in England, when everyone lived off farming and the lords treated their workers well. He was opposed to the recent changes which had produced the industrial towns in which the employers did not care what happened to their workers and their families.

Radical town-dwellers

However, Cobbett also realised that as a result of the growth of towns, the mass of the people were thrown together in their misery, and were more likely to be able to discuss their conditions with their fellow-workers than had been the case when they lived in isolated villages. Writing about his childhood, he said:

As to politics, we were like the rest of the country people in England; that is to say, we neither knew nor thought anything about the matter. The shouts of victory, or the murmurs at a defeat, would now-and-then break in upon our tranquillity for a moment; but I do not remember ever having seen a newspaper in the house. . . . After, however, the American War had continued for some time, and the cause and nature of it began to be understood, or rather misunderstood, by the lower classes of the people in England, we became a little better acquainted with subjects of this kind.

It was only in the towns that men could gather in crowds to hear songs such as:

Come all ye bold Britons wher'er you may be,
I pray give attention and listen to me,
There once was good times but they've now gone complete,
For a poor man now lives on eight shillings a week.
Our venerable fathers remember the year
When a man earned three shillings a day and his beer,
He then could live well, keep his family neat.
Now he must live on eight shillings a week.

Hunt read some of Cobbett's work and became interested in radicalism. In 1810 he was imprisoned along with Cobbett by a government which feared that every criticism of English life was the beginning of a new French-type revolution. When that Revolution seemed to have been defeated and its leader, Napoleon, exiled to St Helena in 1815, the government still tried to restrain anyone who criticised the British political system.

1815 depression

But with the end of the Napoleonic Wars there was a slump in trade, as munitions factories closed down, armies and navies were disbanded, while the new machinery was constantly replacing workpeople in the cotton and woollen industries. Hunt spoke at a huge meeting in Spa Field, London, in 1816 when he declared:

What was the cause of the want of employment? Taxation. What was the cause of taxation? Corruption. It was corruption that had enabled the borough-mongers to wage that bloody war which had for its object the destruction of liberties of all countries but principally of our own. . . . Everything that concerned their subsistence or comforts was taxed. Was not their loaf taxed? Was not their bread taxed? Was not everything they ate, drank, wore, and even said, taxed? . . . [The taxes] were imposed by the authority of a borough-mongering faction who thought of nothing but oppressing the people, and subsisting on the plunder wrung from their miseries.

Here Hunt is attacking both the political system and its effects. The system

15 Viscount Castlereagh, Foreign Secretary in the Liverpool Government until 1822, and popularly thought to be the leading opponent of reform.

allowed men to buy their way into Parliament, as Samuel Romilly remembered:

> I shall procure myself a seat in the new parliament, unless I find that it will cost so large a sum, as . . . it would be very imprudent for me to devote . . . After a parliament has lived little more than four months, one would naturally suppose that those seats which are regularly sold by the proprietors of them would be very cheap; they are, however, in fact sold now at a higher price than was ever given for them before. Tierney tells me that he has offered £10,000 for the two seats of Westbury, the property of the late Lord Abington. . . . The truth is that the new ministers have bought up all the seats that were to be disposed of, and at any price. . . . It is supposed that the king . . . has advanced a very large sum . . . This buying of seats is detestable; yet it is almost the only way in which one who is resolved to be an independent man, can get into parliament. To come in by popular election, in the present state of representation is quite impossible; to be placed there by some great lord, and to vote as he shall direct, is to be in a state of complete dependence.

Under this corrupt system the landowning classes had been able to push through the Corn Law of 1815 which forbade anyone to import foreign corn until the price of English corn rose above 80s (£4) a quarter. This high price benefited the land-owners and their tenant farmers, but it was disastrous for the poorly-paid workers and the thousands who had no work at all.

Reactionary government

Hunt demanded a reform of the electoral and Parliamentary systems so that the

23

16 Henry Addington, Viscount Sidmouth, Home Secretary in the Liverpool Government until 1822. He congratulated the Manchester magistrates on their action at St Peter's Field (Picture 17) and was responsible for the introduction of the Six Acts aimed at checking the activities of the radicals.

ordinary people would have a voice in the election of their government and some control over the laws which it passed. These ideas were totally opposed by the government, which was largely under the influence of Lord Castlereagh.

Shelley wrote the *Masque of Anarchy* in which occur the lines:

> I met Murder on the way
> He had a mask like Castlereagh

In stanza six, Sidmouth was dealt with:

> Like Sidmouth next, Hypocrisy
> On a crocodile came by.

The final rousing cry to the men of England was:

> Rise, like lions after slumber,
> In unvanquishable number!
> Shake your chains to earth, like dew,
> Which in sleep had fallen on you!
> Ye are many – they are few!

Peterloo

The government tried to suppress the radical movement by force. A meeting at Spa Fields in 1816 was dispersed by the yeomanry and in 1817 the march of unemployed Derbyshire workers was dispersed by the army. The Manchester magistrates were following a pattern when a meeting was held at St Peter's Field, Manchester on 16 August 1819. The following account was written less than a week after the event. The banners carried by the demonstrators indicate the nature of their complaints. The yeomanry had been called out by the local magistrates who were afraid that the crowd of 80,000, might cause a riot.

A little before noon on the 16th August, the first body of reformers began to arrive on the scene of action, which was a piece of ground called St Petersfield, adjoining a church of that name in the town of Manchester. These persons bore two banners, surmounted with caps of liberty, and bearing the inscriptions; 'No Corn Laws', 'Annual Parliaments', 'Universal Suffrage', 'Vote by Ballot'. Some of these flags after being paraded round the field, were planted in the cart on which the speakers stood, but others remained in different parts of the crowd. Numerous large bodies of reformers continued to arrive from the towns in the neighbourhood of Manchester till about one o'clock, all preceded by flags, and many of them in regular marching order, five deep. Two

17   The Peterloo Massacre at St Peter's Field, Manchester, 16 August 1819. This engraving was presented to Hunt (on the platform) to commemorate the attack by the yeomanry under the direction of the magistrates seen in the house on the left-hand side of the picture.

clubs of male reformers advanced, one of them numbering more than 150 members, and bearing a silk banner. One body of reformers timed their steps to the sound of a bugle, with much of a disciplined air. . . . A band of special constables assumed a position on the field without resistance. The congregated multitude now amounted to a number roundly computed at 80,000, and the arrival of the hero of the day was impatiently expected. At length Mr Hunt made his appearance, and after a rapturous greeting was invited to preside; he signified his assent and mounting a scaffolding, began to harangue his admirers. He had not proceeded far, when the appearance of the yeoman cavalry advancing toward the area in a brisk trot, excited a panic in the outskirts of the meeting. . . . The cavalry dashed into the crowd, making for the cart on which the speakers were placed. The multitude offered no resistance. The commanding officer then approaching Mr Hunt, and brandishing his sword, told him he was his prisoner. Mr Hunt, after enjoining the people to tranquility, said he would readily surrender to any civil officer on showing his warrant, and Mr Nadin, the principal police officer, received him in charge. . . . A cry now arose among the military of, 'Have at their flags,' and they dashed down not only those in the cart but the others dispersed in the field; cutting to right and to left to get at them. The people began running in all directions; and from this moment the yeomanry lost all control of temper: numbers were trampled under the feet of men and horses; many, both men and women were cut down by sabres, several, and a peace officer and a female, slain on the spot. The whole number of persons injured amounted to between three and four hundred. The populace threw a few stones and brickbats in their retreat; but in less than ten minutes the ground was entirely cleared of its former occupants. Mr Hunt was led to prison not without incurring considerable danger, and some injury on his way from the swords of the yeomanry and the bludgeons of peace officers; the broken staves of two of his banners were carried in mock procession before him. The magistrates directed him to be locked up in a solitary cell, and the other prisoners were confined with the same precaution.

Samuel Bamford, one of the demonstrators wrote:

Within ten minutes from the commencement of the havock, the field was an open and almost deserted space. The sun looked down through a sultry and motionless air . . . the hustings remained, with a few broken and hewed flags staves erect, and a torn and gashed banner or two drooping; whilst over the whole field were strewed the caps, bonnets, hats, shawls, and shoes, and other parts of male and female dress; trampled, torn and bloody. The yeomanry had dismounted – some were easing their horses' girths, others adjusting their accoutrements; and some were wiping their sabres. Several mounds of human beings still remained where they had fallen, crushed down and smothered. Some of these still groaning – others with staring eyes, were gasping for breath,

18 Head of one of the banner poles carried at Peterloo.
(Original in the possession of Middleton Library.)

and others would never breathe more. All was silent save those low sounds, and the occasional snorting and pawing of steeds.

Within the week the Home Secretary wrote to the Lord Lieutenant of the County of Lancashire:

'My lord – Having laid before the Prince Regent the accounts transmitted to me from Manchester of the proceedings at that place on Monday last, I have been commanded by his royal highness to request that your lordship will express to the magistrates of the county palatine of Lancaster, who attended on that day, the great satisfaction derived by his Royal Highness from their prompt, decisive and efficient measures for the preservation of the public tranquillity; and likewise that your lordship will communicate to Major Trafford his Royal Highness's high approbation of the support and assistance to the civil power afforded on that occasion by himself and the officers, non-commissioned officers and privates, serving under his command. I have the honour, etc, *Sidmouth*'

Radical reaction

The government expected that this show of force and the imprisonment of Hunt would diminish the fervour of the radicals. Quite the opposite happened. On 28 August the *Manchester Observer* published a house-that-Jack-built style of poem:

This is the field of Peter-loo. These are the poor reformers who met, on the state of affairs to debate; in the field of Peterloo. These are the butchers, blood-thirsty and bold, who cut, slash'd and maim'd young, defenceless and old, who met, on the state of affairs to debate; in the field of Peter-loo.

This is HURLY-BURLY, a blustering knave, and foe to the poor, whom he'd gladly enslave, who led on the butchers, blood-thirsty and bold, who cut, slash'd and maim'd young defenceless and old, who met, on the state of affairs to debate; in the field of Peter-loo.

These are the just-asses, gentle and mild, who to keep the peace broke it, by lucre beguiled, and sent Hurly-Burly, a blustering knave, a foe to the poor, whom he'd gladly enslave, to lead on the butchers, blood-thirsty and bold, who cut, slash'd and maim'd young, defenceless and old, who met on the state of affairs to debate; in the field of Peterloo.

The Tory government had boasted that it had been responsible for the defeat of Napoleon at Waterloo. The radicals wrote their own poem:

And the heroic host no more shall boast,
The glorious feats of Waterloo!
But this henceforth shall be the toast
The glorious feats of Peterloo!

O would'st thou Albion still be free
And bid to every fear adieu;
Call to thy aid the M.Y.C.
They fought so well at Peterloo!

The ageing radical

Meanwhile Hunt had been sent to gaol for two-and-a-half years. When he was released in October 1822 he continued to speak on radical platforms, contested the County seat of Somerset as radical candidate in 1826 and was finally elected MP for Preston in 1830. But Hunt, the controller of the mob, was unable to adapt himself to life in Parliament where many men were his intellectual equal, many could speak as well as he, and few were willing to sit and listen to him. He was a failure as an MP and the electors of Preston threw him out in 1833. In 1835 he died, aged sixty-two.

Samuel Bamford, who had written so fervently about Peterloo, became more respectable as he got older. During the Chartist demonstration, (Chapter 6), which had many of the aims that Bamford had once supported, he became a special constable. Once again the radical of one generation had become the conservative of the next.

19 The Second Reform Act, 1867, which gave some working men the right to vote in Parliamentary elections, was passed while Disraeli, a Tory, was the leader of the House of Commons. Lord John Russell, the Liberal Leader, is beaten in this race to extend Reform, which by 1867 was not something to be squashed but something that Party leaders fought to introduce.

THE DERBY, 1867. DIZZY WINS WITH "REFORM BILL."

Respectable reform

While Hunt was in prison and later trying to re-establish himself as a leading radical, the cause for Parliamentary reform was taken up by some of the leading Whigs. The aristocratic Lord John Russell, the son of the Duke of Bedford, not only proposed that the whole system should be reformed but managed to persuade the Tory government to disfranchise some of the more obviously corrupt seats (such as Grampound in Cornwall). It was the same Lord John Russell who, as a member of the aristocratic Whig government of 1831, proposed the Reform Bill which became the Reform Act, 1832. That Whig government was led by Earl Grey and included in its number the son of the Earl of Durham, Lord John Lambton who believed that a man 'might jog along on £50,000 a year' thus earning for himself the title 'King Jog'. Hunt and his fellow radicals had been imprisoned for their belief in Parliamentary reform; now the cause of reform had been taken up by the upper classes and in time all that Hunt and his fellow-radicals had asked for would become law. The radical demands of one generation became the accepted ideas of a later one.

29

4 Cobden, Bright and the Anti-Corn Law League

Radical stirrings

William Cobbett, writing about his childhood, remembered the time when people first took an interest in political affairs (Chapter 2). There always has to be a first time for everything – for us personally – and for radicals and reformers. In our own case we know that the first time – for reading, for writing, going to a dance or whatever – happened when we were old enough to do the thing involved. In

20 The artist Cruikshank produced this as his idea of a radical reformer. In the background a small model of the monster singing 'and a *Hunt*-ing we will go' links the monster with the peaceful Hunt. Blood dripping from the knife served to remind the artist's audience that in his opinion, reform could well lead to a French-type revolution with massacres and terrors.

the case of radicals it is exactly the same; a time comes when society, or a part of that society feels that it is old enough, mature enough, to do something different and new. As Macaulay said in 1831:

> History is full of revolutions, produced by causes similar to those which are now operating in England. A portion of the community which had been of no account expands and becomes strong. It demands a place in the system, suited . . . to its present power. If this is granted all is well. If this is refused, then comes the struggle between the young energy of one class and the ancient privileges of another. Such is the struggle which the middle classes in England are maintaining against an aristocracy.

The first generation of newly rich were, like little children, not quite sure of themselves and not accustomed to their new wealth. Their children, however, having grown up with that wealth and in that position were more confident than their parents had been. Their parents had challenged the political power of the aristocracy and had won equality for themselves in 1832. Now the second generation of middle-class industrialists set out to challenge the economic and social power of the ruling, landed class.

Speaking in 1844, Richard Cobden explained his interest in the abolition of the Corn Laws (or free trade in corn): 'We do not expect that it will injure the landowner, provided he looks merely to his pecuniary interest in the matter; we have no doubt it will interfere with his political despotism – that political union which now exists in the House of Commons, and to a certain extent also, in the counties of this country. With free trade in corn men must look for political power rather by "honest means" than by the aid of this monopoly.'

The movement for Free Trade was more than an attack on a trading monopoly; it was also an attack on the whole power of the aristocracy by a new, confident rising middle class.

The Corn Laws
The Corn Law against which Cobden and his League were campaigning was passed in 1815, when Parliament was dominated by the rich aristocrats (Chapter 2) and the government of the day was in the hands of the noble families. They rented out much of their land to tenant farmers who, during the Napoleonic Wars, had been able to pay higher rents out of the ever-increasing prices they received for their produce.

The noble landlords and their tenant farmers feared that the end of the war would see a resumption of foreign trade, with corn being imported from Europe with the result that prices would fall. This in turn could mean lower incomes for the farmers and lower rents (and incomes) for the landlords. To safeguard their own interests they passed the Corn Law, which declared: 'That such foreign corn . . . shall be permitted to be imported into the United Kingdom . . . whenever the price of wheat shall be at or above the price of 80 shillings per quarter [£4]; . . . And be it further enacted, that whenever the price shall be below the price stated, no foreign corn . . . shall be imported into the United Kingdom'.

We have seen that the Peterloo demonstrators had asked for the abolition of the Corn Laws which, as the following contemporary poem shows, made life even harder for the poorly paid and unemployed:

> Ye coop us up and tax our bread;
> And wonder why we pine;
> But ye are fat, and round, and red
> And filled with tax-bought wine.
>
> Thus twelve rats starve while three rats thrive
> (Like you on mine and me),
> When fifteen rats are caged alive,
> With food for nine and three.

Anti-Corn Law League

Anti-Corn Law Associations had been set up in several towns in the 1830s; in 1838 a meeting of representatives of all such Associations was held in Manchester – the industrial capital of the industrial north – and the meeting agreed to set up an Anti-Corn Law League to co-ordinate the work of the various local Associations. These middle-class manufacturers, like their working-class employees, realised that unity is strength; they believed that a national campaign would have more effect than a series of smaller, local campaigns.

The leaders of the League were Richard Cobden and John Bright. Cobden was the fourth of eleven children of a small Sussex farmer. In 1832 he started business as a calico merchant in Manchester and eventually became a manufacturer. John Bright was the son of a Rochdale mill-owner and a Quaker. Together they dominated the League's activities. While they used the traditional radical

21 Cobden addressing the Anti-Corn Law League Council. These respectable, wealthy and industrious members of the middle class had won a share in the country's political system in 1832. They intended to use that political power for their own economic gain and to attack the social power of the aristocracy.

22 John Bright, Cobden's principal ally in the Anti-Corn Law campaign.

methods, meetings, petitions to Parliament, pamphlets, cartoons, songs and the like – they also used more orthodox methods to win their way. Since 1832 the middle class had been allowed to vote in Parliamentary elections. Cobden proposed to use this political reform for his own purpose:

> We propose to keep people well informed as to the progress of our question by means of the penny postage . . . to send them one letter a week, and that will cost twopence for the stamp and the enclosure. That will be £2,500. We intend to visit every borough in the kingdom; . . . we will specially invite the electors to meet such deputations without distinction of party – and having met the electors we shall urge upon our friends to organize themselves, and to commence a canvass of their boroughs to ascertain the number of Free Traders, and in every case where it is possible to obtain a majority of the electors in favour of Free Trade . . . the League will pledge itself, where a borough finds itself at a loss for a candidate, to furnish it with one. [Ours] is not a party move, to serve any existing political organization; we care nothing for political parties. As they at present stand, there is very little indeed to choose between the two great parties. Let a statesman of established reputation, of whatever side in politics, take the step for perfect freedom of trade, he shall have the support of the League.

The League was fortunate in several respects. Without the penny post it could not have sent out its literature cheaply. Without the network of the railway system the leaders could not have travelled around the country, visiting each constituency.

33

The League was supported by the new, wealthy middle class – without their money the League could not have flourished. But above all the League was fortunate in that the 1832 Reform Act had given it the chance to elect MPs who supported the campaign. Cobden himself was elected in 1841; Bright became MP for Durham in 1843. In Parliament they were able to speak in favour of their cause.

The Free Trade movement

The old idea that the nation's industries should be protected from foreign competition by a system of import duties, had been under attack for a long time. In 1776 Adam Smith had written his *Wealth of Nations* as a plea for Free Trade; Young Pitt had removed some duties in the 1780s and Huskisson had moved further towards Free Trade in the 1820s. In the budgets of 1842 and 1844 Peel himself removed many import duties and lowered others. By the middle of the nineteenth century, Britain, the workshop of the world, did not fear foreign competition; her industries did not need protecting. Cobden and the League supported this movement, but carried the argument further. If Free Trade was good for manufactured goods and raw materials, why was it not good for corn as well? Why should Parliament fix the price for only one commodity? In 1844 Cobden said:

> I am a manufacturer of clothing, and I do not know why, in this climate, and in the artificial state of society in which we live, the making of clothes should not be

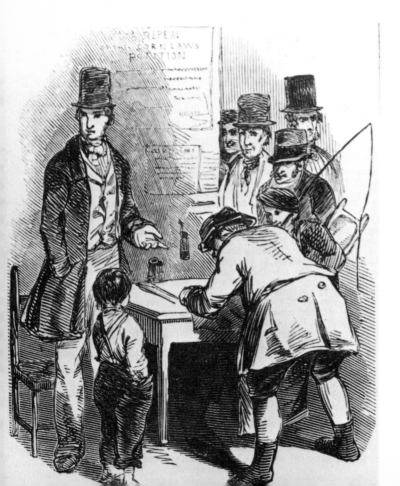

23 Signing the Anti-Corn Law League petition.

as honourable – because it is pretty near as useful – a pursuit as the manufacture of food. Well, did you ever hear any debates in the House to fix the price of my commodities in the market? Suppose we had a majority of cotton-printers (which happens to be my manufacture) in the House. . . . Let us suppose that you were reading the newspaper some fine morning, and saw an account of a majority of the House having been engaged the night before in fixing the price at which yard-wide prints should be sold: 'Yard-wide prints, of such a quality, 10d a yard; of such a quality, 9d; of such a quality, 8d; of such a quality 7d,' and so on. Why, you would rub your eyes with astonishment. Now, did it ever occur to you that there is no earthly difference between a body of men, manufacturers of corn, sitting down in the House, and passing a law enacting that wheat to be so much, barley so much, beans so much, and oats so much?

Why, then, do you look at this monopoly of corn with such complacency? Simply because you and I and the rest of us have a superstitious reverence for the owners of those sluggish acres, and have a very small respect for ourselves and our own vocation.

Radical pacifists
Cobden also believed that Free Trade would lead to a more united and peaceful world:

I believe that the physical gain will be the smallest gain to humanity from the success of this principle. I look farther; I see in the Free Trade principle that which will act on the moral world as the principle of gravitation in the universe – drawing men together, thrusting aside the antagonism of face, and creed, and language, and uniting us in the bonds of eternal peace. I have looked even farther. I have speculated, and probably dreamt, in the dim future – ay, a thousand years hence – I have speculated on what the effect of the triumph of this principle may be. I believe that the effect will be to change the face of the world, so as to introduce a system of government, entirely distinct from that which now prevails. I believe that the desire and the motive for large and mighty empires, for gigantic armies and great navies – for those materials which are used for the destruction of life and the desolation of the rewards of labour – will die away. I believe that such things will cease to be necessary, or to be used, when man becomes one family, and freely exchanges the fruits of his labour with his brother man.

Whig conversion
The force of Cobden's persistent argument finally persuaded the leaders of the aristocratic Whig party that the Corn Laws would have to go. Their leader, Lord John Russell, wrote to his electors in the City of London, 22 November 1845:

'I used to be of opinion that corn was an exception to the general rules of political economy; but observation and experience have convinced me that we ought to abstain from all interference with the supply of food. Neither a government nor a legislature can ever regulate the corn market with the beneficial effects which the entire freedom of sale and purchase are seen of themselves to produce.

Let us then unite to put an end to a system which has been proved to be the blight of commerce, the bane of agriculture, the source of bitter divisions among classes, the cause of penury, fever, mortality and crime among the people.

Let the Ministry propose such a revision of the taxes as in their opinion may render the public burdens more just and more equal; let them add any other provisions which caution and even scrupulous forbearance may suggest; but let the removal of restrictions on the admission of the main articles of food and clothing used by the mass of the people be required, in plain terms, as useful to all great interests, and indispensable to the progress of the nation.

I have the honour to be, Gentlemen, your obedient servant, *J. Russell*'

Peel and Cobden

But what about the Ministry? It was a Conservative Ministry led by Peel, who was pledged to maintain the Corn Laws even though he followed a Free Trade policy in everything else.

Once again fortune favoured the League in two ways. Firstly, Peel was a politician whose record showed him willing to change his mind and policy when he saw that such a change was essential. He had done so over the question of Catholic Emancipation in 1829, even though this had meant splitting the Tory party, bringing down the government and allowing the Whigs in. Again in 1845–46 he was to show a similar strength of character even though the result would be to split his Party once again.

24 *Papa Cobden taking Master Robert for a free trade walk*. Robert Peel later acknowledged the debt he owed to Cobden. *Punch* had understood what was happening before 1846.

25 Starving peasants outside the gate of a workhouse in Ireland in 1846. Peel used this famine as an excuse for repealing the Corn Laws; the repeal did nothing to alleviate the misery of the starving Irish.

Irish famine

Then, again, the League was fortunate that the opportunity was given to Peel to change his mind. In 1845–46 the Irish potato crop – the main food of the Irish peasants – was ruined, so that many thousands died of starvation and millions emigrated to America. Peel used the famine as an excuse to introduce the Repeal of the Corn Laws. Speaking in the Commons on 16 February 1846, he said:

> While I admit that a natural consequence of the courses I have pursued, is to offend, probably to alienate, a great party, I am not the less convinced that any other course would have been ultimately injurious even to party interests. I know what would have conciliated temporary confidence. It would have been to underrate the danger in Ireland, to invite a united combination for the maintenance of the existing Corn Law . . . by such a course I should have been sure to animate and please a party, and to gain for a time their cordial approbation. . . . We were assured in one part of this Empire there are 4,000,000 of the Queen's subjects dependent on a certain article of food. We knew that in that

37

article of food no reliance could be placed. . . . We saw, in the distance, the gaunt forms of famine, and of disease following in the train of famine.

As the Duke of Wellington said: 'It was damned potatoes that did it'. In part Wellington was right – but only in part. Peel himself realised that what he had done was more than a response to a famine; indeed, he knew that no Irish peasant would be saved from death by the Repeal because the peasants had no money to buy corn which, ironically, was being exported from Ireland while the peasants died. Peel knew that the Repeal was a radical change due mainly to the work of

26 A cartoon from *Punch*, 1852. It represents popular opinion of Disraeli's attitude towards protection – which he described as 'dead and damned'. The unfortunate man on the left had really believed in protection; Disraeli and his followers admit that their campaign was against Peel.

THE UNDERTAKERS CAROUSING AFTER THE BURIAL OF PROTECTION.

Cobden. Speaking in the Commons on 23 June 1846, Peel said:

> There has been a combination of parties, and . . . together with the influence of
> the Government has led to the ultimate success of the measures. But, Sir, there
> is a name which ought to be associated with the success of these measures . . .
> the name of a man, who, acting, I believe, from pure and disinterested motives
> has advocated their cause with untiring energy, and by appeals to reason,
> expressed by an eloquence, the more to be admired because it was unaffected
> and unadorned – the name which ought to be and will be associated with the
> success of these measures is the name of Richard Cobden.

After Repeal

Many people believed that the British farmer would be ruined as a result of this
Repeal. Disraeli bitterly attacked his Party's leader for this betrayal of Tory
interests and this submission to the power of the new industrial classes. But when
he himself became a Minister in 1852 it was Disraeli who said: 'Protection is dead
and damned' and he made no effort then, or later when Prime Minister, to restore
the aristocratic monopoly. Once again we see the radical ideas of one generation
becoming the conventional wisdom of a later generation.

5 Shaftesbury, a Radical Nobleman

Some history books give students the idea that all reforms have come about because people from the 'left wing' have agitated, demonstrated and demanded reforms. Such books tell us about the 'great Whig reforms, 1833–41' and 'Gladstone's great reforming Ministry' and 'The Liberals, 1906–14, the founders of the Welfare State'. If we are not careful, we come to think that only the Whigs, the Liberals and later, the Labour Party, provided anything like reforms to help the less well-off. The people who lived through the nineteenth century knew differently. Alexander Macdonald was one of the first working-class men to be elected to parliament. He said: 'The Tories have done more for the working man in six years (1874–80) than the Liberals have done in fifty years.' Reforms come from the right as well as from the left.

Anthony Ashley Cooper was the son of the Earl of Shaftesbury, a title to which he succeeded when his father died. He had had the conventional nobleman's upbringing; educated at Harrow and Oxford University, he had entered Parliament in 1826 as MP for Woodstock in the unreformed parliament where men bought and sold seats (Chapter 3). In 1828 he wrote in his diary: 'On my soul, I believe that I desire the welfare of mankind', and his life's work shows that he tried to live up to this.

27 Lord Shaftesbury.

28 Richard Oastler, 1789–1861, was known as the 'Factory King' in his native Yorkshire. He led the campaign against child-labour in textile mills, comparing the Yorkshire slavery to the evil slavery against which Wilberforce and his friends conducted their campaign. Oastler was typical of many factory owners who were concerned for their workers and their families; many others, however, did not show this concern.

Factory reform

Shaftesbury was a member of the Tory Party. Some Tory landowners had become partners with industrialists or mine owners and had benefited from the industrial changes, which, after 1750, altered the face of England. But most Tory landowners were opposed to the industrial and social changes taking place in England. They disliked the huge, sprawling, dirty new towns where the rate of violent crime was almost as high as the rate of infant mortality. They disliked the new rich class of factory owners who were claiming equality with the upper class (Chapter 4).

In return, Cobden and other members of the rising class of industrialists disliked the old landowning class; one of the by-products of that dislike was the repeal of the Corn Laws (Chapter 4) which made bread cheaper. The working class also benefited from Tory dislike for the factory owners; a series of Factory Acts made life better for working people.

Factory Commission, 1831

Sir Robert Peel, grandfather of the Prime Minister, introduced the first Factory Act in 1802; but this, and later Acts, proposed by Robert Owen and Michael Sadler failed to make life much better for the working class; they relied on the local JPs to inspect factories in their area and to punish factory owners who broke the law. In 1831 young Ashley Cooper took up the campaign for serious factory reform; his Bill was withdrawn when the government agreed to set up the first Royal Commission to investigate conditions of employment in the textile mills in

Lancashire and Yorkshire. The 1831 Commission was the first independent enquiry into the conditions in the 'dark satanic mills' of the North. The evidence shocked the ruling classes:

Evidence of Samuel Coulson:

At what time in the morning, in the brisk time, did those girls go to the mills? In the brisk time, for about six weeks, they have gone at 3 o'clock in the morning, and ended at ten, or nearly half past, at night.

What intervals were allowed for rest or refreshment during those nineteen hours of labour? Breakfast, quarter of an hour, and dinner half an hour, and drinking a quarter of an hour.

Had you not great difficulty in awakening your children at this excessive hour? Yes, in the early time we had to take them up asleep, and shake them, and when we got them on the floor to dress them, before we got them off to their work; but not so in the common hours.

Supposing they had been a little too late, what would have been the consequences during the long hours? They were quartered in the longest hours, the same as in the shortest time.

What do you mean by quartering? A quarter was taken off.

If they had been how much too late? Five minutes.

Were the children excessively fatigued by this labour? Many times; we have often cried when we have given them the little victualling we had to give them; we had to shake them, and they have fallen to sleep with the victuals still in their mouths. . . .

Have your children been strapped? Yes, every one; the eldest daughter . . . when [my wife] came in she said her back was beat nearly to a jelly.

29 Men, women and children working like animals to provide the raw material needed to build up British industrial power. Some people thought that this was too high a price to pay for progress.

What was the wages in the short hours? Three shillings a week each.

When they wrought those long hours what did they get? Three shillings and sevenpence halfpenny [18p].'

Factory Act 1833

As a result of the Commission, Parliament passed the 1833 Factory Act, the first of a series of really effective Acts. Among other things the Act said:

No person under eighteen years of age shall [work] between half-past eight in the evening and half-past five in the morning, in any cotton, woollen, worsted, hemp, flax, tow, linen, or silk mill. It shall not be lawful . . . to employ in any factory . . . as aforesaid, except in mills for the manufacture of silk, any child who shall not have completed his or her ninth year.

It shall not be lawful for any person to employ . . . in any factory . . . as aforesaid for longer than forty-eight hours in one week, nor for longer than nine hours in one day, any child who shall not have completed his or her eleventh year. . . .

It shall be lawful for His Majesty to appoint four Inspectors of factories where . . . children and young persons under eighteen years of age [are] employed, empowered to enter any . . . mill, and any school . . . belonging thereto, at all times . . . by day or by night, when such . . . factories are at work.

Today we may think that this Act was not such a great change; children over the age of nine could still be sent to work in textile mills for 9 hours a day; only four inspectors were appointed to see that the terms of the Act were carried out in the many hundreds of mills set up in Lancashire and Yorkshire; children could work, at any age, in coal mines, engineering shops, brickyards – and, as the Act said, in silk mills.

The 10-hour campaign

The Factory Acts of 1802 (Peel) and 1819 (Owen) had only tried to deal with the working conditions of orphan children; Peel and Owen had not thought it right to try to deal with the working conditions of children whose parents allowed them to go to work. The 1833 Act dealt with the working conditions of children; even Shaftesbury did not think it right, then, to try to legislate for women and men.

Joseph Fielden owned one of Britain's largest factories at Todmorden in Yorkshire; his employees had a 10-hour working day and yet he made very large profits. Fielden, Shaftesbury and others formed a Committee to try to get Parliament to pass a law fixing a 10-hour day as the maximum which could be worked by women and children. They did not try to get Parliament to legislate for male workers; these, after all, were supposed to be able to stand up for themselves. But Shaftesbury and his friends hoped that if the factory owner was allowed to employ women and children for only 10 hours a day then the men would also have to get

a similar 10-hour day since the men could not work without the assistance of the women and children.

The Mines Act, 1842

In 1840 another Royal Commission looked into working conditions first in the mines and then in factories. Once again the conscience of the country was shaken by the reports of conditions in which thousands of women and children worked in the mines, on which so much of Britain's industrial prosperity was based.

Girls regularly perform all the various offices of trapping, hurrying, filling, riddling, tipping and occasionally getting, just as they are performed by boys. One of the most disgusting sights I have seen was that of young females, dressed like boys in trousers, crawling on all fours with belts round their waists, and chains passing between their legs. . . . The Hunshelf Colliery . . . is a day-pit . . . I found at one of the aide-boards, down a narrow passage, a girl of fourteen years of age, in boy's clothes, picking down the coal with the regular pick used by the men. . . .

The practice of employing children only six or seven years of age is all but universal. . . . The children go down into the pit with the men usually at four o'clock in the morning, and remain in the pit between eleven and twelve hours each day. . . . The use of a child up to six years of age is to open and shut the doors of the galleries when the coal trucks pass and re-pass. For this object a child is trained to sit by itself in a dark gallery for the number of hours described.

31 Shaftesbury campaigned for reform in the treatment of lunatics. This is a portion of the *Rake's Progress* by Hogarth and shows the interior of the Bedlam, or a lunatic asylum, to which the former Rake (Picture 6) has now been sent to be ill-treated by other inmates.

By the time this Commission had presented its Report, Peel was once again Prime Minister. Peel distrusted Shaftesbury's over-zealous Evangelicalism and Shaftesbury disliked Peel. In 1841 he wrote: 'Sat next to Peel last Saturday. It was the neighbourhood of an iceberg, with a slight thaw on the surface.' But, as we have seen, Peel was prepared to follow the course which reason pointed out, even if this meant splitting his own Party (Chapter 4).

Shaftesbury and his friends persuaded Peel to pass the Mines Act (1842) which forbade the employment of women in the mines together with that of boys under thirteen. These proposals were bitterly opposed in the House of Lords by Lord Londonderry, one of the industrial-landowners and a great coal-owner.

The 10-hour day

In 1844 Peel passed an Act which regulated the hours of female labour, fixing a 12-hour day for women (similar to that given to young people under 18 by the 1833 Act). Shaftesbury tried to get this amended so that women and young people worked only a 10-hour day. But Peel was supported by most economists and industrialists who believed that the country could not survive foreign competition on a 10-hour day.

In 1847 Shaftesbury and his friends achieved a 10-hour day for women and young persons; the evidence presented by a large number of 'good' employers persuaded Parliament that the country would not be ruined by this move. One employer wrote to Shaftesbury:

> As to the conclusions I have come to from the working of my [mill] for 11 instead of 12 hours each day, as previously, I am quite satisfied that both as much yard and ... cloth may be produced at quite as low a cost in 11 as in 12 hours ... it is my ... intention to make a further reduction to $10\frac{1}{2}$ hours, without the slightest fear of suffering loss. ... I find the hands work with greater energy and spirit; they are more cheerful, and ... happy. All the arguments I have heard in favour of long time appear based on an arithmetical question – if 11 produces so much, what will 12 or 15 hours produce? This is correct [for] the steam-engine, but try this on the horse and you will ... find he cannot compete with the engine, as he requires time to rest and feed.

The reformers hoped that this legislation would force employers to give a 10-hour day to men also; however, employers began a relay system by which no woman was asked to work more than 10 hours a day but some of them were given an hour or two off in the morning, others given an hour or so off in the afternoon, while the factory was kept open for its usual fifteen or so hours with a continuous working day for the men and a 'split' working day for the women and young children. In 1850 Shaftesbury persuaded Parliament to pass an Act which said that women and young children could be employed only between 6 a.m. and 6 p.m., while no man should work more than $10\frac{1}{2}$ hours a day. While the leaders of working-men's associations and unions thought that Shaftesbury had betrayed them by accepting the $10\frac{1}{2}$-hour day, they had to agree that this was a vast improvement on the past.

These early Acts had applied only to workers in textile mills; after 1850 Shaftesbury campaigned to persuade Parliament to extend the terms of these Acts to workers in other industries, such as calico-making, potteries, brewing, engineering and so on. It was not until 1874 that a 10-hour day was finally granted for workers in most industries – and that was an Act passed by Disraeli's Conservative government.

Shaftesbury and the climbing boys

Shaftesbury's humanitarian radicalism was not confined to factory reform. He

32 Children gazing into the window of a shop, August 1910. Shaftesbury had campaigned for children like this – getting them out of the mines and factories, trying to provide them with some schooling and so on. But even Shaftesbury was a prisoner of his times; he could not agree that it was the duty of the state to help provide adequate housing for the poor families from which these children came.

was a partner with Edwin Chadwick in persuading the government to pass the first effective Public Health Act (1848). He was also responsible for changes in the law concerning lunatics who had previously been treated with inhumane cruelty, and was Chairman of the Ragged Schools Union.

Perhaps the most outstanding of his other activities was his campaign on behalf of the climbing boys who were sold at the age of six or seven to a chimney sweep. The beatings that they received to force them to climb the chimneys of the large houses, their deaths from suffocation or lung disease were horrors that were well known. Acts had been passed in 1830 and again in 1864 which said that no one under the age of twenty-one should climb chimneys. Yet the Acts were largely ignored in spite of the impression created by Dickens's *Oliver Twist* and Kingsley's *Water Babies*. Not until 1875 was the law made effective when chimney sweeps had to apply for a licence to practise their trade and the police were given power to take away the licence of anyone who broke the law. After this, the evil of climbing boys soon ceased.

The brief account of Shaftesbury's campaigns for factory and other reforms shows that this was a kindly radical, willing to challenge the accepted ideas of economists, industrialists, writers and others who thought that the government had no right to legislate for working conditions. But Shaftesbury's radicalism was limited in its scope. In 1883 there was a campaign to try to persuade the government to do something about the appalling housing conditions in which over one-third of the British people lived. Some radicals demanded the building of council houses at rents which the poor could afford. Shaftesbury wrote:

If the State is to be summoned to provide houses for the labouring classes, it will, in fact, be an official proclamation that, without any effort of their own, certain portions of the people shall enter into the enjoyment of many good things, altogether at the expense of others.

In 1847 he himself had written a description of a slum;

In the first house that I turned into there was a single room; the window was very small and the light came in through the door. The young woman there said: 'Look there at that great hole; the landlord will not mend it. I have every night to sit and watch, or my husband sits up to watch, because that hole is over a common sewer and the rats come up twenty at a time, and if we did not watch for them they would eat the baby up.'

By 1883 things had got better and not worse, but Shaftesbury's radicalism did not extend to the provision of good, cheap housing. It is as well to remind ourselves that no radical has been in favour of every reform. Cobden (Chapter 4) was opposed to factory reform; Lloyd George was opposed to women's emancipation; Shaftesbury, perhaps the kindest nobleman of them all, was not prepared to allow the government to build decent housing.

6 The Chartists – Working-class Radicals

Working-class protest

The radical changes which have taken place during the past two hundred years have benefited the working class more than any other section of society. The surprising thing is that most of these radical changes have come about because of the activities of middle-class or upper-class leaders. There are few examples of working-class radical activity having any favourable result. The working class has rioted, burned and looted – with the Luddites in the beginning of the nineteenth century and the agricultural riots of the 1830s. But rioting and burning rarely, if ever, lead to a change in society; they usually lead to increased government activity against the rioters and leave life very much as it was before the riot – if not worse.

Radical change requires a systematic campaign to be launched to persuade the government to alter things. This activity depends on people who can see a problem and the ways in which it can be tackled, and can undertake the slow, painstaking process of persuasion. Two examples of such campaigns have already been considered: Cobden and the Anti-Corn Law League (Chapter 4) and Shaftesbury's 10-hour day campaign. In either case did the working class play a significant part.

Middle-class radicalism

In 1831 the middle and the working classes were united in their demands for a reform of the Parliamentary system. The Whigs passed the 1832 Reform Act and admitted the rising middle class to a share in government. The Act did nothing for the working class. The middle class became conservative defenders of property – supporting activities against Trade Unions which led to incidents such as the sentencing of the Tolpuddle Martyrs, and legislation against the poor and unemployed such as the Poor Law Amendment Act, 1834.

The reformed Parliament passed the Poor Law Amendment Act, of which Carlyle wrote:

> Why [does] Parliament throw no light on this question of the working classes? . . . Can any other business be so pressing? . . . A reformed Parliament, one would think, should inquire into popular discontents before they get the length of pikes and torches! Yet read Hansard's Debates! . . . All manner of questions and subjects, except this.

33 This drawing by Phiz shows *Mr Horsfall being murdered by a Luddite gang*. The Luddite movement grew as some men were replaced by machines while others found that their earnings were being cut. Their reaction was a violent one – machines were smashed, factories destroyed and, as illustrated here, factory owners attacked. This is not radicalism but meaningless violence.

Half a million weavers, working fifteen hours a day, [unable] to procure thereby enough of the coarsest food; English farm-labourers at nine shillings . . . a week; Scotch farm-labourers who . . . 'taste no milk, can procure no milk': all these things are credible to us.

The master of horses when the summer . . . is done has to feed his horses throughout the winter. If he said to his horses: 'Quadrupeds, I have no longer work for you; but work exists abundantly over the world; go and seek [it] . . . finally, under pains of hunger, they take to leaping fences; eating foreign property, and – we know the rest.

Carlyle believed that the working class would be bound to revolt because of the cruelty of the new Poor Law and the harsh conditions under which they lived and worked.

The new towns

Most of the workers in the new towns had come from small villages where they and their ancestors had worked on the land and taken part in the domestic system of cottage industry. In these villages there was a known and accepted social structure; the squire lived in his large house: the rest of the villagers knew their rightful place in the social structure – and accepted it. They prayed:

> God bless the squire and his relations,
> And keep us all in our proper stations.

One of the reasons for Tory opposition to the new towns (Chapter 5) was that there was no such obvious and accepted social structure. Cobden and his industrialist supporters went out of their way to challenge this idea that the landed aristocrat was superior to the industrialists. Another reason for this Tory opposition was that the factory owner did not believe that he had any responsibility for the way in which his workpeople were housed, dressed or fed. The squire in the village accepted that this position imposed on him certain duties – to look after the poor, the homeless, the old, and so on. He had an idea that the life of the community was his responsibility. The factory owner had no such idea; he believed that each individual should look after himself. 'Each one for himself' was the industrialists' slogan.

One of the results of this was that the factory owners paid low wages, built poor quality houses, worked people for long hours from an early age – and did not feel guilty. The working people, on the other hand, were the products of centuries of accepting their lowly place in village society, and at first accepted a similarly lowly place in the new society of industrial towns. In *Rape of a Fair Country* Alex Cordell shows how older people (in 1830 or so) opposed their children and grandchildren who were anxious to form Trade Unions, support the Chartists, demand the vote, oppose the employers, and so on. The older people, who still regarded themselves as temporary immigrants from the countryside into the town, were unwilling – perhaps unable – to accept the new ideas that were beginning to attract the support of the workers who knew only the town and were willing to make some attempts to cure the evils that affected their lives.

Trade Unions

In the late eighteenth and early nineteenth centuries some working class men had formed themselves into Trade Unions. At first these were local associations of men employed in the same trade; there were the Bolton weavers, the Sheffield file grinders, the Blackburn carpenters and so on. As methods of communication improved, some ambitious working-class leaders, such as John Doherty, a Lancashire spinner, tried to form a national union of all people working in the textile industry. Others, even more ambitious, tried to form a Grand National Consolidated Trades Union in which every workman would be enrolled, the government threatened by a General Strike unless it passed legislation to improve the living and working conditions of ordinary people.

Such working-class attempts were doomed to fail. The government had allowed

CAUTION.

WHEREAS it has been represented to us from several quarters, that mischievous and designing Persons have been for some time past, endeavouring to induce, and have induced, many Labourers in various Parishes in this County, to attend Meetings, and to enter into Illegal Societies or Unions, to which they bind themselves by unlawful oaths, administered secretly by Persons concealed, who artfully deceive the ignorant and unwary,—WE, the undersigned Justices think it our duty to give this PUBLIC NOTICE and CAUTION, that all Persons may know the danger they incur by entering into such Societies.

ANY PERSON who shall become a Member of such a Society, or take any Oath, or assent to any Test or Declaration not authorized by Law—

Any Person who shall administer, or be present at, or consenting to the administering or taking any Unlawful Oath, or who shall cause such Oath to be administered, although not actually present at the time—

Any Person who shall not reveal or discover any Illegal Oath which may have been administered, or any Illegal Act done or to be done—

Any Person who shall induce, or endeavour to persuade any other Person to become a Member of such Societies,

WILL BECOME

Guilty of Felony,

AND BE LIABLE TO BE

Transported for Seven Years.

ANY PERSON who shall be compelled to take such an Oath, unless he shall declare the same within four days, together with the whole of what he shall know touching the same, will be liable to the same Penalty.

Any Person who shall directly or indirectly maintain correspondence or intercourse with such Society, will be deemed Guilty of an Unlawful Combination and Confederacy, and on Conviction before one Justice, on the Oath of one Witness, be liable to a Penalty of TWENTY POUNDS, or to be committed to the Common Gaol or House of Correction, for THREE CALENDAR MONTHS; or if proceeded against by Indictment, may be CONVICTED OF FELONY, and be TRANSPORTED FOR SEVEN YEARS.

Any Person who shall knowingly permit any Meeting of any such Society to be held in any House, Building, or other Place, shall for the first offence be liable to the Penalty of FIVE POUNDS; and for every other offence committed after Conviction, be deemed Guilty of such Unlawful Combination and Confederacy, and on Conviction before one Justice, on the Oath of one Witness, be liable to a Penalty of TWENTY POUNDS, or to Commitment to the Common Gaol or House of Correction, FOR THREE CALENDAR MONTHS; or if proceeded against by Indictment may be

CONVICTED OF FELONY,
And Transported for SEVEN YEARS.

COUNTY OF DORSET,
Dorchester Division.

February 22d. 1834.

C. B. WOLLASTON,
JAMES FRAMPTON,
WILLIAM ENGLAND,
THOS. DADE,
JNO. MORTON COLSON,

HENRY FRAMPTON,
RICHD. TUCKER STEWARD,
WILLIAM R. CHURCHILL,
AUGUSTUS FOSTER.

G. CLARK, PRINTER, CORNHILL, DORCHESTER.

34 Even though Trade Unionism had been legalised in 1824, respectable opinion was anti-Union. Middle class people preferred to believe that Trade Unions were evil societies – as Cruikshank had persuaded them radicalism was evil (Picture 20). The magistrates who posted this notice, and on the following day ordered the arrest of the Tolpuddle weavers, knew that they had the support of the greater part of middle-class opinion; the Whig government in which Lord Melbourne was Home Secretary supported the decision to arrest and punish the weavers.

Trade Unions to be formed (1824) although it had forbidden them the right to strike (1825), but local magistrates were encouraged to find loopholes in the law to prevent unions being formed.

Chartism

The failure of Parliament to deal with the problems of the working class (see Carlyle above), the growth of the number of working class people who had known no other life except that in the town, the failure of their own attempts to improve conditions via Trade Unions and the 10-hour day campaign, drove some working men to form themselves into local associations set up to demand more parliamentary reform. As early as 1837 the *Dudley Times* had printed the Six Points of the People's Charter:

1 A VOTE for every man twenty-one years of age, of sound mind, and not undergoing punishment for crime.

2 THE BALLOT – to protect the elector in the exercise of his vote.

3 NO PROPERTY QUALIFICATION for Members of Parliament – thus enabling the constituencies to return the man of their choice . . . rich or poor.

4 PAYMENT OF MEMBERS, thus enabling an honest tradesman, working man, or other person, to serve a constituency, when taken from his business to attend to the interests of the country.

5 EQUAL CONSTITUENCIES, securing the same amount of representation for the same number of electors.

6 ANNUAL PARLIAMENTS, thus presenting the most effectual check to bribery and intimidation, since though a constituency might be bought once in seven years (even with the ballot), no purse could buy a constituency (under a system of universal suffrage) in each ensuing twelvemonth; and since members, when elected for a year only, would not be able to defy and betray their constituents as now.

35 William Lovett, a founder of the London Workingmen's Association which was partly responsible for the development of the Chartist movement. Lovett was a 'moral force' Chartist opposed to the 'physical force' group led by Feargus O'Connor.

In one form or another similar charters were drawn up in various parts of the country. In 1836 William Lovett and Francis Place had formed the London Workingmen's Association and branches of this Association were set up in various parts of the country. In his autobiography, Lovett recalled the early days of this Association and its growth into a national movement:

The General Convention of the Industrious Classes originated with the Birmingham Political Union. The Delegates to this body were, for the most part, appointed by very large bodies of men. The Birmingham meeting was composed of 200,000, the Manchester meeting of 300,000, that of Glasgow 150,000 . . . and other towns equally large in proportion to their population. The number of delegates composing the Convention was fifty-three, many of them representing several places. Of this number there were three magistrates, six newspaper editors, one clergyman of the Church of England, one Dissenting Minister and two doctors . . . the remainder being shopkeepers, tradesmen and journeymen. They held their first meeting at the British Coffee House, Cockspur Street, Charing Cross, on Monday February 4th, 1839. . . . On their first assembling the Birmingham delegates proposed me as Secretary, and, though the proposition was at first strongly opposed by some of the physical-force party, I was eventually elected unanimously. This, it would seem, gave great offence to O'Connor. At the next meeting he posted up a notice of motion, by the adoption of which he thought he could get rid of me as Secretary.

The extract reveals the volume of support enjoyed by this Association; it also shows that from its early days there was quarrelling inside the Association, as Feargus O'Connor – the editor of a radical newspaper, the *Northern Star* – tried to impose his will on the Association's members and failed.

In 1839 the Chartists, as they had become known, presented their first petition to Parliament:

That it might please their honourable House to take the petition into their most serious consideration, and to use their utmost endeavour to pass a law, granting to every man of lawful age, sound of mind, and uncontaminated by crime, the right of voting for members to serve in Parliament; that they would also cause a law to be passed, giving the right to vote by ballot; that the duration of Parliament might in no case be of greater duration than one year; that they would abolish all property qualifications, to entitle persons to sit in their honourable House; and that all members elected to sit in Parliament, should be paid for their services.

Parliament rejected the petition – not surprisingly, since an election under the terms of the Charter would have produced a Parliament dominated by working-class voters, one which would legislate for better housing, working conditions, wages, education and so on.

The Chartist movement was not merely a demand for Parliamentary reform; the Chartist leaders realised that any improvement in the lives of ordinary people could only come about if laws were passed. The middle-class Parliament showed no sign of passing such legislation – hence the demand for more reform as a means of obtaining that wider legislation which the workers demanded.

Violence

A second petition was presented in 1842 and again Parliament rejected it. By this time more workers had become frustrated with the orderly attempts at trying to persuade Parliament to listen to reason and extend the franchise to working men. Some, led by the more fiery O'Connor, wanted to use force, to take up arms against the reluctant government. In Preston there were the Plug riots.

These local attempts to use force as a means of gaining their ends were opposed by Lovett and other more patient leaders who saw that the government could not be panicked into giving way. But these same outbreaks of violence frightened the less radical members of society; they might have been persuaded by the logic of Lovett's arguments to support the Chartist movement. Their support would have been enough to force MPs to accept the Chartists' demands and pass the necessary legislation. But the owners of property, the small shopkeepers, the middle-class factory owners, clergymen, journalists and others believed that the Chartist movement was a violent affair which would bring ruin in its wake. They turned against it – and their opinion stiffened the resistance presented by the government.

36 When the local magistrates arrested Henry Vincent and other leaders of the Welsh Chartist movement, John Frost led the miners and ironworkers from the Welsh valleys to Newport where Vincent was in gaol. The army was called out and the clash between the army and the Chartists only convinced moderate opinion that the Chartism was a violent and dangerous affair.

1848 petition

In 1847 the country went through a period of economic slump and high unemployment. The Chartist movement had flourished during such periods in the past; when the level of employment was high only the fervent Chartists came to meetings, and signed petitions. When the level of economic activity was low and unemployment was high, the discontented joined in with the fervent, and the numbers of Chartists grew. O'Connor was elected MP in 1848 and the leaders of the Chartist movement planned a monster demonstration on 10 April in support of yet another petition to Parliament.

The government under Lord John Russell called in the eighty-year-old Duke of Wellington to defend London. Troops were called in and special constables enrolled – including the former radical Samuel Bamford (Chapter 3). The government allowed the Chartists to meet at Kennington Common but forbade them to cross any of the bridges over the Thames. O'Connor, who had addressed the demonstration was allowed to take the Chartists' petition to the Commons. There were six million signatures on the petition which had to be carried in three hansom cabs.

37 Part of the Chartist procession moving towards London, 1848. On the extreme right, in long top coat and carrying a truncheon, you can see one of the hastily-enrolled special constables.

38 The Whig-Liberal government was afraid of a Chartist uprising and in 1848 called upon the Duke of Wellington, the aged hero of Waterloo, to organise the defence of London.

On examination however the government showed that there were in fact only two million signatures and that many of these were forgeries. Some of the signatures were in the same handwriting; others were supposed to be the signatures of Peel, Wellington, Judas Iscariot, and even Queen Victoria. The ridicule that followed almost submerged the movement. On Whit Monday 1848 one group planned to lead riots in suburban London while another group attacked Whitehall, but rain and police action prevented either of the groups getting under way. Another group planned to seize London on 15 August; they were arrested and most of them transported. The final blow to the movement was when O'Connor was declared insane in 1852 and confined to an asylum where he died in 1855. The last great gathering of Chartists was for the funeral of the man who had done so much to wreck the movement.

Chartists and the future
Members of local Chartist associations turned their attention to other methods of improving the lives of ordinary people; some supported the Rochdale Pioneers and the Cooperative Movement; others joined in the development of a strong Trade Union movement which, after 1850, did so much to help the skilled workers to improve their living standards. Others remembered the lessons they had learned at the Chartist Schools and were ready for the works of Karl Marx when these were translated into English in the 1870s. These and other Chartists were founder members of the local branches of the Independent Labour Party founded in the 1880s by Keir Hardie.

57

7 Joseph Chamberlain – a Self-seeking Radical

Radical intentions

When Lord Shaftesbury took up the campaign for factory reform he must have known that he would face many difficulties, many arguments with politicians and writers who believed that the government and Parliament should not take an interest in such matters.

Why did he take up the fight, knowing the difficulties that lay ahead and the probability of failure? There must be many reasons: a humanitarian feeling of sympathy with the oppressed workers, particularly with the children; a dislike for the attitudes of the new factory owners towards their workers; a religious belief that people in positions of power should use that power wisely and for the benefit of the lower classes. One thing can safely be said: Shaftesbury did not take up the campaign in the hope that it would help him to get on in life; the campaign for the climbing boys was not a step towards promotion for himself.

Chamberlain (1836–1914)

Joseph Chamberlain had joined his cousin, Joseph Nettlefold, in running a Birmingham screw business. In a very short time he had built up the firm so that it provided most of the screws, nuts and bolts bought by British industrialists. While still young, Chamberlain was rich enough to retire from business and devote himself to public life. He brought the same drive and energy to politics that he had shown as a business man; he founded the Birmingham Liberal Association, the first attempt at the formation of an organised political party anywhere, and after he and his friends had won enough seats on the Birmingham Council, in 1873 Chamberlain was elected Mayor, an office which he held until 1876 when he entered Parliament. During those three years Chamberlain, in his own words, 'parked, paved, gassed [lighting] and watered and improved' every street in the city. The radical Mayor and his friends made Birmingham cleaner, healthier, and the example to all other councils of how a vigorous, free-spending council could do away with the slum horrors of the industrial towns. This campaign did not make him popular with landlords of slum property or with the richer ratepayers, neither of whom gained from this policy.

In 1876 he became MP for Birmingham along with John Bright (see Chapter 4) and within a short time had made his impact on national politics. His attacks on the aristocracy and the monarchy earned him the title of 'Republican Joe' – and the hostility of the Tories, the Lords and the ageing Queen Victoria. His

39 Joseph Chamberlain speaking at Bingley Hall, Birmingham in 1904, during his Tariff Reform Campaign. He is holding up a 'Free Trade loaf' and a 'Tariff Reform loaf' and asking his audience whether they can see any difference between the two. Birmingham, Chamberlain's constituency, remained loyal to him but throughout the country as a whole his campaign only served to split the Tory party and help the Liberals to gain a huge majority.

attacks on Disraeli's foreign policy with its wars in South Africa, its dangers of wars in Egypt and Turkey, made him the darling of the pacifist radical-left, but the enemy of the patriotic, flag-waving majority of the British people. He helped to lead the campaign for free and universal education in state schools where no catechism should be taught; this earned him the hostility of the Anglican Church and its political partner the Tory Party, with its majority in the House of Lords.

In 1880 the Liberals formed a government under Gladstone, himself something of a radical in the eyes of his supporters and enemies, and in the eyes of his followers the fount of all wisdom. But Chamberlain, the brash rising radical, was not prepared to pay the Grand Old Man the homage that was due to him; Gladstone said:

40 Waiting for food parcels at Cheapside, London in 1901. About one-third of working men earned less than £1 a week and lived in dire poverty; about one-tenth of the country's men were unemployed at this time and received no help from the state. For the poor there was charity such as that illustrated here, or the workhouse.

There is a disposition to think that the Government ought to do this and that, and that the Government ought to do everything. If the Government takes into its hand that which the man ought to do for himself, it will inflict upon him greater mischiefs than all the benefits he will have received. . . . The spirit of self-reliance should be preserved in the minds of the masses of the people, in the minds of every member of that class.

Against this, Chamberlain, the rising, ambitious leader of a small group of radicals was arguing:

It is therefore perfectly futile and ridiculous for any political Rip Van Winkle to come down from the mountain on which he has been slumbering, and to tell us that these things are to be excluded from the Liberal programme. . . . We have to account for and to grapple with the mass of misery and destitution in our midst. . . . I shall be told tomorrow that this is Socialism. . . . Of course, it is Socialism. The greater part of municipal work is Socialism, and every kindly act of legislation by which the community has sought to discharge its responsibilities and its obligations to the poor is Socialism, but it is none the worse for that. Our object is the elevation of the poor, of the masses of the people.

The Liberals split

There is an obvious clash between the almost pre-Victorian ideas held by the ageing Gladstone and the almost twentieth-century ideas of the brash young man who was so bold as to call Gladstone 'Rip Van Winkle'. In 1886 – a year after Chamberlain's speech, quoted above – Gladstone was once again Prime Minister, for the third time. Without consulting his Cabinet he announced that the Liberal government, including Chamberlain and Bright, would spend most of its time on forcing through a Bill to give Home Rule to Ireland. Chamberlain realised that this would be unpopular with the country and would lose the Liberals a good deal of support; he also realised that if the government spent its time on this Bill, then none of the 'socialist' reforms which he wanted would be put into practice.

He resigned from the Cabinet and sat in the Commons as the leader of a group of about forty MPs who were opposed to Gladstone, who supported the Union between Britain and Ireland, and who became known therefore as Liberal-Unionists. Perhaps he hoped that the majority of Liberal MPs would follow him

41 One of the causes of rising unemployment was the decline of Britain's share of world trade. The 'workshop of the world' had tended to rest on its laurels. Other countries, such as Germany (shown here) and the USA, had developed their industries and were taking trade away from Britain.

CAUGHT NAPPING!

| THERE WAS AN OLD LADY AS I VE HEARD TELL, | SHE WENT TO MARKET ON A MARKET DAY | BY CAME A PEDLAR—GERMAN—AND STOUT, |
| SHE WENT TO MARKET HER GOODS FOR TO SELL, | AND SHE FELL ASLEEP ON THE WORLD'S HIGHWAY. | AND HE CUT HER PETTICOATS ALL ROUND ABOUT. |

42 Joseph Chamberlain's constituency produced this postcard as a souvenir of the 1906 Election during which Chamberlain celebrated the thirtieth anniversary of his entry into Parliament in 1876. Imperial pride rivals pride in the city of Birmingham with the slogan 'forward Birmingham', while industrialism struggles with socialism in the slogans at the bottom of the card.

so that he could become the leader of the Liberal Party and so, one day, Prime Minister. Perhaps he hoped that in time the Liberal Unionists would imitate the Peelites after the split of 1846. After all, Gladstone had been a member of a splinter group in 1846 and yet he had become Prime Minister; why should this not happen to Chamberlain?

By 1895 the Liberal Unionists had supported the Conservatives led by Salisbury throughout their government (1886–1892) and had opposed Gladstone's government when the ageing politican became Prime Minister for the fourth but brief time in 1892. When Salisbury became Prime Minister again in 1895 he invited several leading Liberal-Unionists to become Ministers; Chamberlain was offered a choice of posts and, surprisingly, took the relatively minor post of Colonial Secretary. And so the former 'Republican Joe' joined hands with the Party of 'Queen and Country'; the man who had argued against religious education in schools joined the Anglican Conservatives; the man who had opposed Disraeli's adventurous foreign policy entered a Cabinet led by Disraeli's former Foreign Secretary, Lord Salisbury.

The Boer War

This was not the end of his conversion from radical republicanism to radical imperialism. Within a short time of taking office, Chamberlain was in touch with Cecil Rhodes, the millionaire Prime Minister of the Cape Colony who believed that 'we are the finest race in the world, and the more of the world we conquer the better it will be for the world'. Rhodes, as a first step towards this British-dominated world, wanted to control the route from the Cape to Cairo – where the British already controlled Egypt.

Chamberlain, as Colonial Secretary, was responsible for the actions of the colonial governments in the Cape of Good Hope and he supported Rhodes' plan for an attack on the two republics by an armed force from the Cape. The attack failed (1895); Rhodes had to resign as Prime Minister but Chamberlain continued to follow Rhodes' policy of aggression against the Boers. In 1899 the Boer War broke out, its main aim being the acquisition of the gold and diamond fields of the Transvaal and the securing of the trade route from the Cape to Cairo. The radical politician who had opposed Disraeli's African policy had now gone many steps beyond anything dreamed of by his former opponent.

The Conservative split

At first the war was a disaster for the British, but by 1902 the Boers had been defeated, the Conservative government re-elected by a grateful, conquering

43 *Sons of the Blood*, a painting by S. Begg, was produced to commemorate the victory over the Boers in 1899–1902. Chamberlain, as Colonial Secretary, carried the responsibility for the declaration of war, and earned the gratitude of the nation when the war was won.

electorate, and Chamberlain was a hero. But he wanted to become more than a hero of the second rank. Salisbury had resigned and his place had been taken by his nephew, Balfour, who kept Chamberlain on in his Cabinet as Colonial Secretary.

By this time Britain had lost its place as the world's leading industrial and trading nation. The United States of America was producing more coal and steel than Britain; Germany was producing more steel, and rapidly overhauling Britain in the production of coal. Both Germany and the USA, France and Japan, were becoming successful exporters of manufactured goods into markets which had previously been dominated by British firms.

One of the results of this decline was rising unemployment; another was a fall in the profits being earned by industrialists and by investors in British industry. Chamberlain decided to support the campaign for the abolition of the Free Trade system under which Britain allowed foreign goods to enter the country without paying any taxes, although foreign countries imposed import taxes on any goods entering their countries, so making it more difficult for British exporters.

And so once again, the rising, ambitious politician resigned from the Cabinet when Balfour, the Prime Minister would not agree to support Chamberlain's campaign for Tariff Reform. Chamberlain's mind was made up; Britain had to abandon Free Trade and begin a system of Tariffs which would protect her industries. Poor Balfour was less sure. The Canadian Prime Minister wrote at the time:

44 *Gaining Ground.* The title of this cartoon was taken from the speech by an official of the Tariff Commission when making a presentation to Joseph Chamberlain. The great cause of Tariff Reform, said the official was 'steadily gaining ground'. As the cartoon shows this optimism was misplaced; the campaign crunched to an end in the election of 1906.

I'm not for Free Trade, and I'm not for Protection.
I approve of them both, and to both have objection.
In going through life I continually find
It's a terrible business to make up one's mind.
So in spite of all comments, reproach and predictions,
I firmly adhere to Unsettled Convictions.

In 1886 Chamberlain had resigned because Gladstone would not follow the more radical line; the Liberal government fell and the Conservatives entered on almost twenty years of government. In 1903 Chamberlain resigned from the Conservative government; a weaker, disunited Conservative Party lost the election of 1905–6 and the Liberals entered upon a period of government. The next Conservative government would not appear until 1922. Once again Chamberlain had done for his party.

Conclusion

From this brief examination of the work of Joseph Chamberlain, several things stand out. It seems that a radical politician cannot be contained within the confines of the normal political party; his ambitions, the compulsions that force him to begin and continue a campaign make it impossible for him to behave as the normal party-politician has to behave. The normal party man knows that he cannot have everything he believes in and is satisfied if he can get some of his ambitions realised. The radical has to have all or nothing, even if this means splitting the party in which he grew up.

It also seems that a radical of the Left may very well become a radical of the Right. Chamberlain, the opponent of war, became the great war-maker of 1899–1902. Lloyd George's career indicates the same sort of conversion for, having vigorously opposed Chamberlain's Boer War, Lloyd George went on to become the successful leader of Britain's Great War against Germany.

But above all, Chamberlain's career shows that the radical is often right even if he is right about fifty years too soon. In his demand for a more radical socialist policy Chamberlain was right; one of the results of the failure of the Liberals to follow Chamberlain's policy was the growth of the then infant Labour Party which had 1 MP in the Parliament elected in 1900, 29 MPs in the 1906 Parliament, 43 MPs in the 1910 Parliament and which, by 1923, had grown so that Ramsay MacDonald became the first Labour Prime Minister. It is possible that if the Liberals had become socialist-minded, as Chamberlain wanted, then there would have been no room for a Labour Party to grow.

On the matter of Tariff Reform, the future again proved that the radical had been right. After the failure of his campaign (1903–6) to convert the Conservative Party and to win support at the General Election, Chamberlain's health broke down and he retired from active politics, although he retained his seat in parliament until he died in 1914. His son, Neville, held several posts during the Con-

45 Ramsay MacDonald, the first Labour Prime Minister, speaking at the Labour Victory demonstration in the Albert Hall in 1924. The photograph shows MacDonald, Miss Margaret Bondfield, the first woman Cabinet Minister, J. H. Thomas, leader of the National Union of Railwaymen and a future Colonial Secretary, and Robert Smillie M.P. In part they owed their place on this platform to the failure of the Liberals to adopt Chamberlain's socialist policies.

servative governments in the 1920s and in 1932 he was Chancellor of the Exchequer in a Coalition government that had been formed to try to cope with the gigantic problem of the Depression in which 3 million were unemployed. On 4 February 1932, described by Neville Chamberlain as 'the greatest day of my life,' he went to the House of Commons, took his notes from the red dispatch box which had been his father's as Colonial Secretary, and announced that Britain was at last going to give up Free Trade, was going to impose import taxes on foreign goods coming into Britain, in the hope that this would help British manufacturers, trying to sell their goods in the home market. He ended his speech with a tribute to his father:

> There can have been few occasions when to the son has been vouchsafed the privilege of setting the seal on the work which the father began. Nearly 29 years have passed since the great campaign in favour of Imperial Preference. More than 17 years have gone by since he died, convinced that, in some form, his vision would eventually take shape. His work was not in vain. Time and the misfortunes of the country have brought conviction to many. I believe he would have found consolation for the bitterness of his disappointment if he could have foreseen that these proposals would be laid before the House of Commons in the presence of one and by the lips of the other of his sons.

The 'other of his sons' was Austen Chamberlain, also an MP, who came down and shook his brother's hand while the House 'cheered and cheered again' – for the memory of the radical who had at last and again been proven right.

8 Women Radicals – Early 'Women's Lib'

When Queen Victoria came to the throne in 1837, men and women of all classes accepted the idea that man was a superior being, meant by God and Nature to dominate the world, while woman was meant to obey and serve. Joseph Ashby, the agricultural reformer, came from a working-class home; his daughter writes: 'Their mother would teach them, always by action and sometimes in words, that girls and women find it best to submit to husbands and brothers. Their duty was to feed them well, to run their errands and to bear for them all burdens save physical ones. . . . Of course the main source of the doctrine on women was Father's head!' Independence or 'separate action' for women would be 'false, foolish, destructive of women's best and holiest qualities'.

The middle-class family was run on exactly the same lines; the bearded, confident, dominating father (Picture 46) illustrates the point.

46 A comfortable, middle-class family in Norwood, London, 1900.

Women and work

Throughout the nineteenth century working-class women were expected to raise a large number of children, as well as continue to work to supplement the family income. Many thousands were employed in factories, brickyards (Picture 1), laundries, and in trades like dressmaking; in the countryside large numbers of women worked in the fields, particularly at harvest time. But the main single form of employment for women was domestic service. The number of household servants rose from about three-quarters of a million (in 1840) to nearly one and a half million by 1914.

Middle-class women, on the other hand, were not expected to go to work. Educated in private day schools or at home by governesses, they were expected to marry someone of their own class, raise a large number of children and superintend the running of a home staffed by a large number of servants.

But for about one-quarter of these middle-class girls there could be no marriage as young bachelors emigrated to one or other of the colonies or died in wars in Africa, or Asia. And anyhow, some women preferred, and many still do prefer, not to marry. What did life hold in store for the single, middle-class girl? Some became companions to their 'luckier' sisters or sisters-in-law and helped to bring up other people's children: some took up 'good works' and helped parsons and priests to run societies to help the poor.

The right to work

Working-class women had never had to campaign for the right to work; indeed for many of them, marriage to a skilled worker, regularly employed at a good wage, meant an escape from the drudgery of work in factory or field. It was the pampered middle-class women who demanded the right to go to work. Florence Nightingale was fortunate when, in the 1840s, she decided to take up a career in nursing; her parents agreed to support her – many other middle-class parents would have strongly opposed such an idea. Elizabeth Garrett was equally fortunate in having the support of her parents when she decided, in the 1860s, to become a doctor. They supported her in her struggle with the English medical authorities who refused to allow her to train in hospital, or sit examinations; they backed her when she studied to qualify first as an Apothecary, then as a student at the Paris medical school where she obtained her doctor's certificate in 1870.

It was determined women such as these who helped to found the *Gentlewomen's Journal*. This magazine tried to show women that there was a life outside marriage, that there were things they could do other than become governesses, or companions to elderly ladies. But unless girls were as well educated as boys, the number of jobs open to them was limited. In the second half of the nineteenth century Miss Buss and Miss Beale and other pioneers helped to provide greater opportunities for middle-class girls who wanted to become more educated, while Miss Emily Davies founded the first women's College at Cambridge (Picture 47). However, for most Victorian fathers – and mothers – education was something meant for

47 A demonstration against the admission of women to the University of Cambridge, 1897. The middle-class males, then at the University reflected the opinions of their parents that 'there is no place for you maids'.

boys only. Sir Lawrence Jones who went to Eton and then to Balliol, Oxford, writes:

> Equality of opportunity was not yet a political, far less a domestic, slogan. Thousands of other families were economising on the girls to send one bright boy to College. But, in looking back across fifty years, my gratitude for all that was lavished on myself is a little clouded by the reflection that generosity rather than justice went to the shaping of my good fortune. And had I been one of my sisters, I should, I think, have felt the unfairness of it. To have been wholly untrained for the world would have seemed to me a high price to pay for being kept unspotted by it.

The highly educated girls leaving the schools opened by Miss Buss or the University College opened by Miss Davies, might hope to imitate Elizabeth Garrett and become doctors. The less well educated middle- and lower-middle-class girls found increasing opportunities for work as a number of changes took place in Britain. The development of new inventions such as the telephone (Picture 48) and the typewriter, opened up job opportunities for many thousands. As the government became increasingly active in the field of social welfare, so there was a demand for more civil servants and jobs were available for women. As industrial firms became larger they needed head offices and administrative staffs – including some women. The spread of state education provided opportunities for thousands of women teachers, while the opening of large shops – such as Selfridge's in London – was another development providing work for women.

In 1901 eighteen per cent of all clerks were women; by 1911 the percentage had risen to thirty-two. By 1901 there were 212 women doctors and 140 dentists. By 1910 women could become accountants – but not barristers. Middle-class women were on the march for work.

48 The telephone exchange at St Paul's churchyard, London. Job opportunities for middle-class women were provided by technological developments, including the telephone and typewriter.

Votes for women

Not until 1870 did Parliament allow a married woman to keep whatever money she might earn; only in 1882 did Parliament decide that wives be given the right to own property and give it to whom they wished – previously, a married woman's property automatically became her husband's.

As Parliament slowly and reluctantly allowed women these rights, and industry, commerce and government provided increasing opportunities for women to go to work, some radical women began to agitate for equality of opportunity to vote. In the 1850s the radical MP John Mill used to introduce each year a motion for granting women the right to vote in Parliamentary elections. Each year the motion was rejected by a male Parliament which was reluctant to alter the balance of nature – as they saw it. After 1888 women could vote in local government elections; after 1907 they were even allowed to become councillors. Mrs Garnett Fawcett founded the National Union of Women's Suffrage Societies to coordinate the work of the many local Suffrage Committees that had sprung up all over the country. Her Union believed that as women became more free – to work, own property and so on – Parliament would have to recognise the justice of their claim to the vote. Mrs Fawcett and her followers believed that it was only necessary to keep pointing this out in lectures, pamphlets and petitions, for Parliament to give way one day.

Many men and women did not believe this. Some formed themselves into the Women's Anti-Suffrage Committee, in which Joseph Chamberlain (Chapter 7) was a leading figure. Others, on the other hand, joined the Women's Social and Political Union founded by Mrs Emmeline Pankhurst in 1903. Mrs Pankhurst's followers believed that women would only get the vote if they protested and demonstrated in a violent fashion; these 'Suffragettes' heckled at political meetings (Picture 49), chained themselves to railings at Downing Street and Buckingham Palace, smashed shop windows, slashed valuable pictures at art galleries, cut telephone wires and burned public buildings – all to draw attention to their case. As Dangerfield recalled:

And so the WSPV ceased to interest itself in the delicate complicated and patient game of working up a non-partisan majority in the Commons. Christabel Pankhurst had touched some profound instinct in every one of its members. The women must get together, they must fight shoulder to shoulder against the

49 A scene at the Albert Hall in December 1908 at a meeting of the Women's Liberal Federation which Lloyd George addressed on the subject 'Women's Suffrage'. Miss Ogston, a militant supporter of Mrs Pankhurst, was in a box and armed with a whip. When the stewards came to take her out because of her heckling, she lashed out furiously. She had chained herself to her seat and was dragged out only after a violent struggle in which 'respectable gentlemen' assaulted 'respectable women'. What was the world coming to?

enemy. . . . It was the Government they must aim at, and the Government was clearly most vulnerable on the question of property; property therefore must be threatened. 'The argument of the broken window pane,' Mrs Pankhurst declared at a dinner given to released prisoners on 16 February, 1912, 'is the most valuable argument in modern politics. And at this particular effort of feminine reasoning, the authorities groaned in spirit, thinking of London's infinite miles of valuable plate glass.

And well might they groan! At 4 p.m. on the afternoon of 1 March, a meeting at Scotland Yard deliberated on the best methods of protecting shop-keepers from the Suffragettes, and at 4 p.m. on the same afternoon, little groups of women, expensively dressed and carrying large fashionable bags, drifted with perfect nonchalance into the West End. Piccadilly and the Haymarket first resounded to the smashing of glass; thither rushed police and pedestrians, and women with hammers in their hands (flints, it had been discovered, were inclined to bounce off the best plate glass) were the centre of little groups. These accompanied them, in considerable excitement, all the way to the police station. But scarcely had the last offender been bundled safely inside, when once again the sound of ruined glass splintered the evening air. This time it was Regent Street and the Strand which suffered. The police hurried off to these new centres of destruction, and no sooner had they rounded up the culprits, than the windows of Oxford Circus and Bond Street crashed in their ears. Upon that crowded and brilliantly lighted quarter, there descended a rattling darkness, as shutters were fitted and iron curtains came down on the ruins. Tall commissionaires peered out into the streets, gazing with an angry but wincing eye, upon any unaccompanied female, if she happened to carry a bag or a parcel. But all these precautions were in vain. The tactic of ruining in relays worked perfectly, and the ordered destruction went on until half past six . . . until the damage had mounted into thousands of pounds.

Many women, and the majority of men, thought that their campaign had to be stopped. Demonstrators were arrested and imprisoned; when prisoners went on hunger strike they were forcibly fed while the police were encouraged to break up meetings violently. As Mary Richardson recalled: 'I shall always remember the hateful, weasel face of one man in the mob. Like his fellows, he wore a lock of a woman's hair in the buttonhole of his lapel – they wore our hair like trophies in their coats in those days.'

Women and War (1914–18)
The militant campaign organised by Mrs Pankhurst and her daughter Christabel was called off when war broke out in 1914, and the Suffragettes demanded 'the right to serve'. In the forces, on the farms and in the factories they helped to win the War (Picture 50). In 1918 Parliament was asked to consider a Reform Bill which would give the vote to more men – about half the working men in the

50 Girls, including women members of the Forces, waving flags during the celebrations following the Armistice, 1918. Having served, would they now be allowed to vote? Only if they were 30 years old.

country did not yet have the right to vote. This provided an opportunity for some Radical MPs to persuade Parliament to give the vote to some women. As Lord Birkenhead recalled, when speaking to the House of Lords in 1928:

[In 1918] I was against the extension of the franchise to women. I am against the extension of the franchise to women. I shall always be against the extension of the franchise to women. . . . It was in the year 1918, after the War, that the disaster took place. Had it not been for the War in my judgement we should have continued successfully to resist this measure for an indefinite period of time. But what happened?

51 Polling day 1929, and Captain Ian Fraser, the blind Conservative candidate, secured the votes of the 'flappers' as the newly enfranchised 21-year-old women were called. At last women had the same political rights as men.

Let me describe to your Lordships, how gradually, yet now inevitably, we descended the slipping slope. First of all it was not proposed that women should be included. Then a member of the House of Commons, and an important one, said that whoever was included or was not included, it was quite impossible to exclude from the franchise the brave men who had supported our cause in the field. . . . That argument in the spirit of the moment was accepted with facile enthusiasm, and accordingly the soldiers were admitted, subject to the qualification of age and without reference to any other very rigorous examination. Then another member of the House arose and said: 'If you are extending the franchise to our brave soldiers in recognition of their valour on the field how about our brave munition workers . . .?' That argument too was difficult to resist when once you had yielded to the first. Then an insidious and subtle member of the House said, 'How about our brave women munition workers?' And having once on principle yielded to the first argument, it was absolutely impossible to resist the second. . . .

Freedom

In 1918–19 Parliament removed the barriers to women becoming members of the legal profession; in 1923 the first of a series of Divorce Acts was passed, making it as easy for a woman as for a man to end a marriage. The increasing use of contraceptives meant that women had smaller families; the increasing development of gadgets meant that it was easier to run a home in the 1930s than it had been before, and since 1945 an ever-increasing number of women have managed to combine their two roles of job-and-home.

Today we see nothing strange about women being appointed to posts of Cabinet Ministers (Picture 45), or judges, of women being journalists or scientists. While only a few support the violent campaign for Women's Lib there are even fewer who suggest that we should return to the Victorian past, with its male-dominated society. The women radicals did their job well.

9 Oswald Mosley and Right-wing Radicalism

There is some evidence that most demands for great, or radical, changes come from the left wing of politics. Robert Owen in the 1820s and 1830s wrote and talked about a social Utopia; Hunt, (Chapter 2) was among the leaders of the first radical demand for Parliamentary reform, also seen as a means to a better life for everyone; Chamberlain (Chapter 7) began his political life as 'Republican Joe', the socialist enemy of the aristocracy and the monarchy.

In one way this is not surprising; the less well-off members of society and those who speak for them naturally want changes in society; the better-off are much more likely to want to conserve or preserve things as they are. Not surprisingly there are few examples of radical changes being proposed by the better-off, right-wing politicians.

The 1920s and 1930s

It is difficult for us today to believe that life in the 1920s and 1930s was ever as confused and depressing as it obviously was. The War (1914–18) had a many-sided effect on Britain's political, social and economic life. It encouraged the movements towards democracy – in 1918 all adult males and many adult females were given the vote (Chapter 8); it allowed many working-class people to experience and demonstrate leadership for the first time: in the forces, or in one of the many industrial councils set up by war-time government. Men and women who had tasted these fruits of freedom were not likely to submit easily to domestic service and the cap-touching that had been the norm before the War.

In 1916 Harry Gosling the President of the TUC said 'We hope for something better than a mere avoidance of unemployment and strikes after the war'. The more ambitious working class were led by outstanding men such as Ernest Bevin of the Transport and General Workers Union. They had their own Labour Party, grown from the minnow of 1900 to the giant of 1923 when Ramsay MacDonald became the first working-class Prime Minister.

But in spite of this change in the social climate the country's economic position was desperate; old, decaying industries, unable to compete with the newer, more mechanised coalmines and steelworks of the USA, Japan and Germany, found that in a world of shrinking trade they were unable to employ as many men as they had done in 1913. Harry Gosling's hopes for less unemployment were doomed after 1920. Until 1939 Britain never had less than one and a half million

52 October 1924 and a dole queue outside a Labour Exchange. Having fought a war and been promised a country 'fit for heroes to live in' about two million men were unemployed – and neither the Conservatives nor the Labour governments seemed capable of doing anything to help.

men out of work while between 1929 and 1933 the number of unemployed remained above three million.

The end of a system?

To many people it seemed that the capitalist system which had created the industrial power of Britain and other countries was breaking down. Throughout the world the picture seemed the same; in the USA, Germany, Australia – everywhere the numbers of unemployed remained at a depressingly high level. Karl Marx, writing in the 1860s, had prophesied that the capitalist system would one day come down in ruins; in the 1920s and 1930s many believed that the day had come, and in their hour of despair turned to Communism as an apparent solution to their economic problems.

Certainly it seemed that the normal democratic parties had no answer to the problems. A Conservative government, under Stanley Baldwin, and a Labour government led by Ramsay MacDonald, took turns at holding office from 1923 to 1929. Each claimed to have the solution to the problem of unemployment; each lost power with the number of unemployed higher than when they had first entered office. In 1931 the Labour government fell apart under the pressure of the economic crisis and MacDonald invited Baldwin and the Liberal leader, Herbert Samuel, to join him in forming a National government.

In 1926 the TUC had called the General Strike and for nine or ten days the workers in a number of industries ceased work. The government was saved by the middle class, which provided enthusiastic volunteers to drive buses and trains, deliver milk and bread, and do many of the jobs previously done by the workers. The leaders of the left wing such as A. J. Cook – the miner's leader – felt that they had been betrayed by their social superiors. In the 1930s the movement towards the Communist Party was led by men and women from this same middle class. Perhaps their experience of work had taught them that the workers had grounds

53 The formation of the National Government was quickly followed by a General Election in 1931. This government promised to do something to help the unemployed—but failed.

for discontent; perhaps it was the sight of the long dole queues that persuaded them to support the Communists. Whatever the reason, the 1930s saw a number of outstanding young men and women of the privileged middle and upper classes helping to lead the move towards the left.

Meanwhile in Europe the level of unemployment remained high and the normal democratic parties proved incapable of coping with the problem. In Spain the people turned, in the early 1930s, to the parties of the extreme left in the hope that their socialism would help them to provide a solution; in Italy, the King – Victor Emmanuel – called on Mussolini to form a Fascist government in 1922, and Europe saw the first experiment in right wing radicalism. In 1932 the Nazi Party became the largest single party in the German Parliament and Adolf Hitler, a former house painter and ex-army corporal, was invited to become Chancellor (or Prime Minister).

Hitler promised social reforms, measures to end unemployment and a recovery of German pride and prestige. Within a short time he had greatly reduced unemployment by a policy of public works including the building of the giant motorways, and rearmament.

54 An anti-Fascist salute being given by British members of the International Brigade on their return from Spain where they had been fighting against the Franco uprising.

55 Mosley and his Blackshirts marching through south east London in 1937. The police protected the marchers from possible attacks from the Jews living in the area who were the target for Mosley's anti-Semitic speeches.

Britain's right wing

Oswald Mosley, the son of a wealthy family, had been educated at Winchester and at the Royal Military College, Sandhurst. He had married the daughter of Lord Curzon, a former Viceroy of India and a member of the Women's Anti-Suffrage League (Chapter 8). After service during the War, Mosley became Conservative MP for Harrow in 1918, but quickly became disenchanted with the government which did little for the unemployed. In 1922 he left the Conservative Party and, after sitting as an Independent MP for two years, he joined the Labour Party and became MP for Smethwick in 1926. In 1929 MacDonald appointed him to be one of the committee of three, with special responsibility for unemployment.

The Labour Minister with special responsibility for unemployment was former Trade Union leader J. H. Thomas. Like most of his fellow Ministers, Thomas had no idea of what to do in the face of the economic crisis. Mosley, intelligent and concerned, produced a programme that was sensible and constructive – but was too sweeping for his elders who turned his ideas down. He resigned from the government in protest and appealed to the Labour Party's Annual Conference to support him against the leaders who had proved incapable of producing any solution to the problem of mounting unemployment.

But Party loyalty was too strong, and the unemployed members of the Labour Party preferred to support the sterile policies of MacDonald and Thomas rather than the more imaginative policies of the impatient but brilliant Mosley.

In 1931 he and a group of his followers left the Labour Party to form a new party; for a time he was supported by active leftists such as Aneurin Bevan and Stafford Cripps, but after his party had failed to win a single seat at the 1931 election (Picture 53), these left him to return to the surer grounds of the Labour Party. Mosley and his followers then founded the British Union of Fascists. To attract attention and support, Mosley – like other radicals before him – held meetings and organised demonstrations. Like Hitler, Mosley blamed the world's economic problems on Jewish bankers and industrialists and his marches through London's East End – the home of many Jews – became increasingly violent and aggressive. The Communist party helped the Jews to defend themselves and bitter street fighting often took place.

Mosley could afford to pay for huge halls for mass meetings of his supporters. A newspaper account of one meeting reads:

London's Fascist Defence Force turned out in full strength, well briefed and trained to the task of the evening. Its members were swelled to thousands by contingents from as far north as Liverpool. Many of these wore kid gloves containing knuckle-dusters or heavy rings; in many a trouser-pocket, 'black-jacks' lay ready to hand; they were to take up positions in groups of half a dozen or so at all points in the Olympia amphitheatre – round the arena and the tiered gallery which rose from it. . . . On the slightest interruption from any part of the hall a signal would be flashed. Immediately Mosley, standing in dramatic isolation on the vast stage, would cut off his harangue. The battery of twenty-four loudspeakers, capable of drowning a great chorus of hecklers, would fall silent. Powerful searchlights stationed near the stage would focus their full glare instantly on the interrupter. The nearer squads would move into action while the rest of the Blackshirts round the hall would set up a roar of 'We Want Mosley – Mosley'.

Two extremes

In Europe the struggle between the two extremes – the left wing Communists and the right wing Fascists – dominated the political scene in the 1930s. In Italy, Spain and Germany the right wing won the struggle; elsewhere, as in France, the struggle continued until Petain and Laval led a right wing government which

81

56 Mosley at the head of a Fascist May Day Rally in 1938. In spite of heavy unemployment and the failure of various governments, the British people never rallied to Mosley, as the Germans had done to Hitler.

accepted a peace with the conquering Germans. Britain alone was saved from the effects of such a struggle. In *The Glory of Parliament*, Harry Boardman, Parliamentary reporter, recalling Stanley Baldwin, wrote:

For this country a conflict of the two extremes of Left and Right could be avoided if his own party, the strongest in the State and embracing the Right, would have the wisdom and courage to shift to the centre ground of a liberalised Toryism. A Non-conformist divine congratulated him on one of his recent emollient speeches on industrial relations. 'Well,' answered Mr Baldwin, 'I am opposed to Socialism, but I have always endeavoured to make the Conservative Party face left in its anti-Socialism.' He was the born champion of the middle way given to England at a time when, history may pronounce, she most needed it.

It seems that the common-sense of the British people which rejected the left wing solution offered by the General Strike was also capable of rejecting the right-wing solution offered by the brilliant, ex-officer, dark-haired and moustached Mosley. Radical movements may succeed (as did the movements led by Hunt, Chamberlain, Cobden and others) provided that the radicalism is within the main-stream of British tradition – for equality, freedom, equal rights and so on. When the solution proposed by the radical of the left or right is outside that main-stream the British people have tended, in the past, to reject it. Mosley tried to win working class support by calling attention to the presence of the Jews among the population of London's East End. He failed; it is to be hoped that subsequent radicals of the right, basing their appeal on the grounds of the presence of coloured people will have the same lack of success.

War (1939) and its aftermath

The war between Britain and Germany saw the end of the radical movement led by Mosley (Chapter 9); he and many of his chief assistants spent the war in internment. The experience of the 'lonely years' – 1940–42 – when Britain stood alone against Hitler, created a spirit of national unity and a new attitude to social change. In the 1930s the peace-time government had seemed incapable of dealing with the social problems of unemployment and poverty; the wartime government started a National Milk scheme to provide cheap milk for expectant mothers and

57 Sir William Beveridge, the father of the modern Welfare State, speaking at the Albert Hall in 1946.

young children (July 1940), provided free cod liver oil and orange juice at Welfare clinics (1941) and in June 1941 appointed a Commission, under Sir William Beveridge, to examine the existing social insurance system and to make recommendations for its improvement.

Beveridge said: 'Now, when war is abolishing landmarks of every kind, is the opportunity of using experience in a clear field. A revolutionary moment in the world's history is a time for revolutions, not for patching.' In December 1942 he produced his Report which argued that the five Giant Evils of Want (or poverty), Disease, Ignorance, Idleness (or unemployment) and Squalor (from bad housing), could be overcome by government action. As part of that action he proposed that the government should set up National Insurance and National Health Schemes (Picture 57).

In 1944 a government White Paper promised to use every means to see that there was never a return to the large scale unemployment of the 1930s (Chapter 9). In 1945 the British people elected a Labour government to implement the radical changes outlined in these various Papers and Reports. Between 1945 and 1949 the country went through 'the greatest social revolution in its history' according to a speaker at the Conservative Conference (1949). Today's children, born into the modern Welfare system, cannot fully appreciate the nature of this revolution as a result of which everyone had a job, wages were continually increasing, sick people received free and full attention, old people were given adequate pensions and every child had the opportunity of going on to higher education.

An American once told Beveridge that the Welfare State would make the people 'soft and lazy'; he said that if there had been social security in the days of Elizabeth I there would have been no Raleigh, Drake or Hawkins. Beveridge's reply was 'Adventure came not from the half-starved, but from those who were well-fed enough to feel ambition'. Freedom from want was the privilege of a minority in the reign of Elizabeth I; in the reign of Elizabeth II, which began in 1953, this freedom was extended to everyone.

One result of this new and popular freedom was the emergence of a new radicalism which challenged accepted attitudes and codes of behaviour.

Radicalism reappears

In 1956 John Osborne's play *Look Back in Anger* was produced at the Royal Court Theatre. *The Times* critic said: 'The piece consists largely of angry tirades. The hero regards himself, and is clearly regarded by the author, as the specimen of the younger post-war generation which looks around the world and finds nothing right with it.' This generation wanted social change and improvements and they believed that they had been let down by a Labour government which had run out of steam by 1949 and which had been replaced by a Conservative government in 1951. Although their elders thought that the country had experienced the 'greatest social revolution in its history', the young were still dissatisfied. They saw that the existence of the aristocracy and the House of Lords, control of industry by a minority of the population and the re-appearance of a Conservative government indicated that things were very much as they had always been.

Osborne's was the first indication of the emergence of the 'Angry Young Men' who challenged the basic ideas of their elders and rulers. While the play was running at the Royal Court, Sir Anthony Eden's Conservative government embarked on the Suez War by which they hoped to regain control of the Suez Canal, overthrow President Nasser of Egypt and show the world that Britain was still as great a country as in the past. The country was more divided than it had ever been; radical students clashed with students supporting the aggressive policy of the Eden government; in pubs and clubs, schools and factories, shops and homes the argument raged – many people believed that the Eden policy was in keeping with our imperial traditions while others believed that it was a last ditch attempt by a failing nation to assert its greatness (Picture 58).

Nuclear disarmament

The Suez war divided the nation and led to anti-government demonstrations such as the country had never seen before. Many younger people questioned the right

58 Thousands of people attended a Labour Party meeting held in Trafalgar Square in November 1956 to protest against the government's attack on Egypt. This was the first of the massive demonstrations which have since become part of London's life.

59 Youthful supporters of the CND movement wearing the CND badge. From this movement many young people learned the habit of civil disobedience.

of a government to act in this way – and this was a step on the road to the questioning of all authority, which has been a feature of the national life since 1956. One of the most significant examples of that challenge to government authority was provided by the Campaign for Nuclear Disarmament (CND).

In 1950 the Attlee government had decided to spend £1,500 million a year on armaments as part of the anti-Russian policy common to all western European nations. Many people believed that this was more than the country could afford. In 1953 Russia tested her first hydrogen bomb and the Conservative government decided that Britain too must have a hydrogen bomb. Immense sums of money and a large slice of the nation's scarce technical resources were spent on the development of rockets; as one after the other the much-praised rockets failed, many people began to question the wisdom of spending money in this way.

Other people questioned the morality of weapons much more powerful and destructive than those which the Americans had dropped on Hiroshima in 1945; some of these people were pacifists who had always believed that war of any sort was wrong. Others believed that while there might be a case for using 'conventional' weapons, with their limited power of destruction, there was no case for using nuclear weapons which had an unknown power for destruction. They argued that a nuclear war between the major powers would lead to the destruction of the world as we know it.

60 Terry Chandler (left) and Mike Nolan (right) in canoes, getting a warning from an officer as they approach the *Patrick Henry*, one of the American supply ships at the *Polaris* submarine station at Holy Loch, Scotland.

Others were drawn to support the Campaign because they wished to lessen American influence in Britain. Right-wing Conservatives resented the way in which the American government had helped to force the British government to withdraw from Suez and become the laughing-stock of the world; left-wing radicals resented the thousands of Americans stationed on bases in Britain, who appeared to be using Britain as a sort of aircraft carrier in their watch on the Russians.

In 1958 the organisers of the Campaign led a march of their supporters from London to the Atomic Research Establishment at Aldermaston (Picture 59). About 50,000 people took part, many dropping out as the march got further from London. In the following year the Easter March began at Aldermaston and ended in a rally in Trafalgar Square, when over 100,000 joined in its closing stages. Local CND committees sprang up all over the country and local demonstrations and meetings were held. Nationally, the leaders were divided – as had been the Chartists (Chapter 6) – into those who wanted to carry on a moderate campaign against nuclear weapons and a more violent group, the Committee of One Hundred, who tried to organise a campaign of civil disobedience. Supporters were invited to stage rallies of protest in such a way that traffic was disrupted, government business impeded, and the nation's attention brought to the Campaign. (Picture 60).

The Labour Party and the Campaign

One of the leaders of the CND was Frank Cousins, general secretary of the country's largest Trade Union – the Transport and General Workers' Union. At the Labour Party Conference in 1960 there was a debate on whether Britain should remain a nuclear power or not. Hugh Gaitskell and most of the leaders of the Labour Party argued that Britain had to have nuclear weapons; otherwise, they said, Britain would have no influence over the USA and Russia. Frank Cousins led the attack against this policy, and succeeded in winning a victory over the official leadership of the Labour Party. The organisers of CND hoped that this victory would lead a future Labour Government to accept their arguments and give up Britain's nuclear weapons.

The Labour Party Conference of 1961 reversed the decision, accepting the Gaitskell argument, and the CND failed to maintain its hold over the Labour Party. The Campaign, which had never won widespread approval, began to lose the support of the faithful, many of whom drifted to other radical movements.

61 In 1962 the Americans carried out a number of nuclear tests. In Britain thousands of people were against this policy, and many took part in a sit-down demonstration outside the American Embassy in London.

The sight of Earl Bertrand Russell leading a series of protests against government policy, of Labour MPs such as Michael Foot marching alongside Canon Collins and other clerics, lent weight to the anti-authoritarian spirit of the time. If it was in order for a noble earl, descended from former Prime Ministers, to challenge the government of the day, it was presumably in order for lesser beings to challenge the lesser authorities with whom they came in conflict. In the 1960s Beveridge's argument was now to be proved true: the young people of the 1960s had grown up in the comfort and shelter of the affluent, Welfare society which, with all its drawbacks, provided the vast majority with work, high wages, and a standard of living that seemed unbelievable to older people brought up in the 1920s and 1930s (Chapter 9). The post-war generations came to accept full employment, high wages, a state social system, as rights and not as privileges; indeed, they went a number of steps further and demanded many other rights

62 A confrontation between the police and marchers protesting against American participation in the Vietnam War.

63 On the tenth anniversary, anti-apartheid sympathisers in London re-enact the 'Sharpeville Massacre' in which white South African police shot coloured demonstrators.

which the existing system was not willing to concede (Picture 61). Young radical students demanded a share in the running of their universities and colleges; when this was refused, they imitated the CND, organising demonstrations and sit-ins, until authority conceded many of their demands. In the 1970s no university or college authority would try to treat students as they had been treated in, say, 1950; indeed, many of these authorities try to keep one step ahead of their radical students by making concessions which the students have not yet begun to demand. Once again we see that the radical ideas of one generation become the conventional wisdom of the next.

Young students, fresh from the successful challenge of their college authorities, formed the nucleus of the radical demonstrations against the American participation in the Vietnam War. In 1962 and 1963 mass rallies were organised by the supporters of Ho Chi Minh and the Vietcong against the policies of the Johnson government. This was part of a world-wide pattern of anti-American demonstrations, and it may have helped to play a part in changing the USA policy in Vietnam (Picture 62).

Other radicals supported the anti-apartheid movement, protesting against the treatment of black people in South Africa. In 1968 the South African government refused to allow the MCC to take a coloured cricketer – Basil d'Oliveira – on their tour of South Africa where he had been born and from which he had emigrated to try to lead a fuller life in Britain. The MCC called off the tour and the young radicals were encouraged to try to stop the tour of Britain by the South African Rugby team in the winter of 1969–70. However, the tour took place in spite of massive demonstrations; radicals clashed with the police and rugby followers and this helped to draw attention to their cause. One result of this was that the MCC cancelled the tour which the South African cricketers were supposed to make in the summer of 1970. The young radicals had succeeded in changing the MCC committee's mind on this matter and their example encouraged others – in Australia similar demonstrations led to the cancellation of the proposed tour by the South African cricketers in 1971. One effect of these challenges to the White South African policy has been the demand, by white South African sportsmen, for a change in their government's policy. They are afraid of being isolated from the rest of the sporting world, and they want their government to relax its anti-apartheid laws to allow coloured sportsmen to compete on equal terms with white sportsmen. If this happens it will be a major breakthrough for black South Africans and a major victory for the young radicals.

64 Bertrand Russell, the 88-year-old Earl and descendant of Lord John Russell (Picture 19), being given a helping hand as he climbed on to the base of the Nelson Monument in Trafalgar Square, London, to make a speech in favour of nuclear disarmament. If Beveridge was the father of the modern Welfare State, Russell could have claimed to be the father of the modern radical movement, since he led the CND campaign.

Conclusion – Features of Radicalism

We have seen that Britain has experienced, and is experiencing, a number of radical movements. Some people have been frightened by the appearance of yet another radical campaign; George III tried to halt Wilkes (Chapter 2); the Tories tried to stop Hunt (Chapter 3); and others have tried to prevent the success of radical movements.

But later generations have accepted quite calmly the demands of the older radicals; women now vote and the country has not been ruined (Chapter 8); children no longer work in coal mines or factories, yet industry still prospers (Chapter 5). We see that the fears of the opponents of the radicals were not justified. Indeed, we have seen that the once-radical demand becomes an accepted part of the nation's life.

It might be argued that a nation which did not experience radical movements from time to time was an unhealthy nation; just as there are conflicts and arguments in a healthy family, so there should be in a healthy society. The only place where there can be no argument or quarrel is a graveyard; perhaps it is true that only dead, moribund nations have no radical movements.

Every radical movement has been a reaction against the conditions of society as seen by the existing radicals. Human society can never, of course, be perfect; we must therefore expect people to react against its imperfections and demand the righting of evils – such as children being exploited (Chapter 5) or women being treated as second-rate citizens (Chapter 8). A wise government recognises this, and while it tries to put off the day when the radicals' arguments have to be accepted, it does not try to ignore the arguments completely. Less wise governments try to stamp out the radical movement, as did the Russians in Hungary (1956) and Czechoslovakia (1968). As Macaulay said, 'history is full of revolutions' arising from such attempts at strangulation of legitimate radicalism.

How many people in the 1970s can remember the CND demonstrations (Chapter 10)? How many recall the student demonstrations which affected the universities and colleges in the late 1960s? Every radical movement is similarly short-lived and once the radical demands are met, the nation settles down to digest the change, and life goes on much as before.

But if the individual radical movement appears to be short-lived, radicalism as such continues to be a feature of the healthy society. The ripples from the fading CND movement helped to generate the next wave of young radicalism (Chapter 10). As this fades in its turn there will undoubtedly be other radical movements.

Which of our institutions – such as Parliament (Chapters 2 and 3), laws (Chapter 4), conditions (Chapter 5) or minorities (Chapter 8) – demand the attention of the new radicals? Only the future, and not history, can tell.

FURTHER READING

General histories of the period are useful; also the *Human Documents* series by E. Royston Pike, and *English Historical Documents*, published by Eyre and Spottiswoode in several volumes.

Amongst the economic histories which illuminate the times are: *A Social and Economic History of Britain 1760–1950*, by Pauline Gregg; *The Industrial Revolution*, by T. A. Ashton; *The Workshop of the World*, by J. D. Chambers; *Great Britain from Adam Smith to the Present Day*, by C. R. Fay.

Particular topics are dealt with in: *The Peterloo Massacre*, by J. Marlowe; *The Anti-Corn League*, by N. McCord; *The Great Hunger*, by Mrs Cecil Woodham Smith; *Living Through the Industrial Revolution*, by Stella Davis; *The Chartist Movement*, by Mark Hovell; *The Imperial Tradition and its Enemies*, by A. P. Thornton; *The Edwardians*, by J. B. Priestley; *Woman*, by Katherine Moore.

The lives of some of the personalities are recorded in: *The Life of William Cobbett*, by G. D. H. Cole; *Disraeli*, by R. Blake; *Victorian People*, by Asa Briggs; *Gladstone*, by Sir P. Magnus; *My Life*, by Oswald Mosley; *Power and Influence*, by Sir William Beveridge.

Index

95